Big Book
of
Green Smoothies

by
Robyn Openshaw

Big Book of Green Smoothies

Published by Robyn Openshaw/GreenSmoothieGirl.com
Lindon, UT
February 2011

ISBN 978-0-9831113-6-8

Printed in the United States of America.

Disclaimer

Nothing in this book is intended to claim to diagnose, treat, cure, or prevent any disease. This book is not a substitute for primary medical care, but should be seen rather as an educational resource.

Trademarks

All trademarks mentioned are the property of their respective owners.

Contents

GreenSmoothieGirl Readers' Smoothies

Robyn's Smoothies

About the Author

Robyn Openshaw grew up the eldest of eight children, raised on a tight budget where the menu was dominated by simple plant foods: whole grains and legumes, greens, fruits and vegetables, and nuts and seeds.

She has a Web site, GreenSmoothieGirl.com, with tens of thousands of new visitors monthly, dedicated to helping people achieve high energy and vibrant health. Its mission is to teach families how to live a whole-food lifestyle (mostly plants and 60-80% raw) diet that is easy, inexpensive, and delicious—in addition to nourishing.

Robyn taught at a university and now lectures all over the U.S. She is the author of the *12 Steps to Whole Foods* course, *The Green Smoothies Diet*, and several recipe books. She is also the author of two children's books, *The Adventures of Junk Food Dude* and *Junk Food Dude's Yummy Healthy Recipes*.

She is a single mom of four competitive athletes with high-caloric needs who help develop and test her recipes. She received undergraduate and graduate degrees from Brigham Young University and the University of Utah and she loves "arranging the elements" in the kitchen, reading and writing, cycling, running, and competitive tennis.

Acknowledgments

Recipe preparation: Desirée Ward

Desirée prepared the recipes that Katie photographed. She is my first-ever co-author, for *Healthy Holiday Favorites*. Her Web site featuring whole-food and gluten-free cooking is www.unconventionalkitchen.com. Contact her at desiree@unconventionalkitchen.com.

Food staging & photography: Katie Dudley

Katie is a genius with food photography, which isn't an easy subject. I know tons of photographers but recruited her specifically to shoot my recipes. Contact her at katie_dudley03@yahoo.com.

Editing & page design: Deb Tokarewich

Deb is a language master par excellence and nonpareil, with a fine eye for detail. (I'm a former editor and know good from better from best; thus I hire only the finest.) She also loves playing with templates, fonts, graphics, and other page design stuff. Contact her at dtokarewich@yahoo.com.

Cover design: Alana Mae Jenkins

Alana Mae's cover beat 169 other designs in a contest because I fell madly in love with her creation—it's feminine and fanciful, artistic and attention grabbing. Contact her at southcoastdesigner@hotmail.com.

Introduction

I did not invent the green smoothie. I believe they've been around a long time, and Victoria Boutenko coined the term and began to popularize them. I read her book *Green for Life* when it came out and was very excited to follow her recommendations. The content of the book was wonderful. But I felt that good recipes were needed.

My site, GreenSmoothieGirl.com, which teaches people to eat a whole-foods diet, has had 80,000 visits a month in 2010. So I have lots of amazing readers of my blog and newsletter. They have great ideas well tested on families and picky eaters, so I went to them for their favorite recipes. This collection is a compilation of many GreenSmoothieGirl.com reader favorites, as well as my own.

What blender should I buy?

I am a big fan of investing in a turbo blender. Mine are the most important thing I own, the single best tool in my whole-foods kitchen. Green smoothies can yield such massive health benefits, you might as well have a blender that can handle fibrous stalks of greens, frozen fruit, and ice. It's also an incredible tool for making healthful frozen desserts, salad dressings with puréed ingredients like onions and garlic, raw soups, seed/nut pâtés, and much more. For a comparison of blenders, see http://www.greensmoothiegirl.com/robyn-recommendations/blenders/best-blender/.

That said, if you cannot afford a turbo blender right now, please use whatever blender you have to get started. You may just not be able to use frozen fruits, stalks of your greens, and very much ice. Your smoothies may not be particularly smooth. But give it a try with what you have, until you've saved enough, rather than miss out on the opportunity to start an exciting habit that improves your health.

What is the yield for the recipes?

The recipes here vary in their yield. A few that were contributed by readers include yield amounts, but most do not. My personal recipes yield six pints and are most easily made in a large (96 oz.) BlendTec container.

If you have the smaller, 64 oz. container that comes with your machine, you can still use large-batch recipes, but your container will fill up before you've added all the fruit called for in the recipe. You can just blend as much of the ingredient list that fits in the container until smooth and pour half of the mixture out into your glass jars. Then add the rest of the fruit, blend again, and pour the remainder into the jars. Put a lid on the jars and shake well.

But if you prefer smaller batches, just cut the recipes in half for a yield of approximately three pints.

I developed the large-batch, six-pint (three-quart) recipes for a family's needs, or for one person doing the three-day detox plan. At my house, I use this batch for a quart daily for me, and a pint daily for each of my four children. I maximize how much I can get out of the blender, filling it very full.

Keep in mind that if three quarts are too much for you, you can save green smoothies for the next day. (That's as long as they'll last, though. By the third day, they'll have lost a lot of nutrition and will taste funky, too.)

I highly recommend owning the largest container (96 oz.) for the BlendTec and making these large batches, even for a single person. A single person can drink a quart that day, save a quart for the next day, and freeze a quart for a third day. This way, you're cutting your time and effort by two thirds for the same benefit. It'll make a big difference in your ability to get excellent nutrition within your busy schedule. Instead of spending 10 minutes in the kitchen daily, a single person can spend 10 minutes every *third* day. Just remember to get the frozen smoothie out several hours before you want to use it—and shake it well before drinking.

Why is spinach in most of the recipes?

I use spinach in most of these recipes. One reason is that it's not only high in protein, but also outstanding in virtually all nutritional measures. A more practical reason, though, is that it's easy to have spinach on hand. Costco sells huge, 2.5 lb. bags of spinach at the time of this writing for $3.95, as well as more expensive tubs of organic baby spinach. Using lots of spinach helps keep smoothie costs low. (Use other greens for taste as well as that all-important vitamin and mineral variety.) So, considering simplicity for my readers, I include spinach as the last green you add to a recipe to achieve the maximum greens-to-fruit ratio. However, you can always substitute a different green in any recipe.

Why are GreenSmoothieGirl recipes (at the end of this collection) grouped by seasons?

I have grouped my own recipes by seasons to indicate when the ingredients for those smoothies are most likely available in grocery stores in the U.S. You may be able to find each season's ingredients available in other seasons as well—but this way, for your grocery shopping plans, you can quickly identify recipes that are sure to have ingredients available at the time of year you're shopping.

How can I make this easier and cheaper?

Some people get a green smoothie club started at work. The office can pool funds to buy a high-powered blender for the company break room, as well as greens and fruit for the week. Then those in the group take turns making green smoothies for everyone. I would imagine if the employer knew the health gains (see my research in *The Green Smoothies Diet*), he or she might consider sponsoring such an effort! After all, 85% of regular consumers experience more energy.

I met two GreenSmoothieGirl.com readers, who came up to me at a car wash, who have an interesting arrangement worked out. Karri is single and has more time than money, and Bo has a family and has more money than time. So Bo pays for the ingredients, and Karri makes the smoothies every day and delivers some for Bo and her husband. This is problem solving and community mindedness at its best.

How can I help others develop a green smoothie habit?

Several times, when friends of mine have been ill or recovering from surgery, I have asked what I can do to help. And my friends have said, "Could you just make me green smoothies?" Eventually I realized that was something I would do for them that no one else would, so I start with that, rather than the generic, "What can I do?"

People appreciate a plate of brownies, of course—but not as much as something you do for them that helps rather than hurts them in the long run. A green smoothie can help them recover more quickly, feel better, and lose weight if that is needed—or gain weight, if a chronic mineral deficiency causes underweight.

The more we can help each other develop these positive health habits to replace the negative ones, the more we build positive karma. And that good karma just flows to you in so many ways.

Another idea was contributed by reader "mgm" on my blog. She blends "reds" (cabbage, carrots, berries, etc.) and pours it in a pretty glass. Then she blends "greens" (with banana and a little agave) and pours it in a thin stream into the red mixture. The result is a pretty swirled drink of rainbow colors. She also has pretty shot glasses to pour her coworkers a sample. Don't underestimate the power of making it pretty and fun.

Also see "10 Tips for Getting Kids to Go Green" in my book *The Green Smoothies Diet* and the intro of *12 Steps to Whole Foods* about how to deal with reluctant spouses and kids.

Where is my recipe and/or child's photo?

All recipes contributed by my readers have an attribution line directly beneath the recipe title. The recipes are organized alphabetically according to the contributors' names (*not* by the recipe names). Only first names (and last-name initials, when known) are noted.

Many of my readers also responded to my request to send in photos of their children enjoying green smoothies. These delightful pictures are the end of the reader-contributed recipes section, and they also are organized alphabetically by the children's names. First name and state or country are noted next to each.

GreenSmoothieGirl Readers' Smoothies

My Readers' Creative, Healthful Smoothies!

Baby's Beautiful Bountiful "B" Blend
Thanks for the recipe, Adrienne!

This was the first green smoothie that my girls liked. I have been incrementally increasing the amount of spinach. They love the very dark purple color from the blueberries.

> 1-1½ C frozen blueberries
> 1 frozen banana
> 1 small handful spinach leaves

Blend and enjoy!

Peachy Green
Thanks for the recipe, Ali K.!

> 1 serving Vega protein supplement (packed with Omega-3s, perfect amino acid profile, all raw, vegan)
> 4 C spinach *or* 2 C kale
> ½ banana
> 2 peaches
> 1 tsp. stevia
> 1 C water
> 2 C ice
> chlorella tablet (for more greens!)
> maca tablet (for stamina)

Blend and enjoy!

Bee Happy Smoothie
Thanks for the recipe, Alicia G.!

    2 large handfuls romaine lettuce
    2 large handfuls spinach
    ½ lemon
    1 banana
    1 Tbsp. coconut oil
    1 tsp.-1 Tbsp. bee pollen
    water to desired consistency
    optional: 1 handful frozen berries

Blend and enjoy!

Alyssa's Favorite
Thanks for the recipe, Alyssa!

    2 C homemade kefir
    3 handfuls spinach or any other greens in season
    1 banana
    1 Moroccan preserved lemon wedge (fermented)
    1 pinch dulse sea weed
    3 Tbsp. coconut oil
    ¼ C coconut milk
    1 ml. cod liver oil

Put all ingredients except coconut oil in blender and blend. Continue blending and add the coconut oil (if you put it in with all the other ingredients at the start, it will solidify since the kefir is usually cold).

This the "base." Then I add fresh or frozen fruit—whatever I have on hand or whatever I am in the mood for—until it hits the 4 C mark on the blender. Continue blending until smooth.

My favorite fruit to add to the above base:
    pineapple and a little more coconut milk (makes a piña colada-ish drink)
    blueberries, to hide the green color (a blueberry smoothie)
    mixed fruit from Sam's Club (a mixed-fruit smoothie)
    mixed berries from Sam's Club (a mixed-berry smoothie)

I take this to work in the morning, pop it in the freezer there for 1 hour, and when I take it out, it is very frothy and frozen. Yummy!

Banana Split Smoothie

Thanks for the recipe, Ambre S.!

> 1 C kefir
> 1 bunch spinach
> 1 bunch kale
> 1 large spoonful natural peanut butter (we use Smucker's)
> 1 spoonful cocoa powder
> 2 frozen bananas
> 1 handful frozen strawberries
> ¼ C pineapple
> 1 Tbsp. prepared chia gel
> 1 Tbsp. flax meal
> shake of powdered kelp
> shake of fenugreek powder

Blend until smooth.

Banana Breakfast Smoothie

Thanks for the recipe, Andrea!

> 2 bananas, peeled
> 1-2 handfuls fresh curly parsley, washed
> water

Add all ingredients to blender, then blend well. I usually pour some into a screw-top beaker for work and drink the remainder for breakfast.

Mouthwatering Mango Smoothie

Thanks for the recipe, Andrea!

> 1 large mango, peeled and sliced
> 1-2 handfuls fresh spinach, washed

Blend the mango and spinach together well. If you prefer your smoothies to be thinner, add some water to desired consistency and blend again.

Green Machine

Thanks for the recipe, Andrea M.!

Makes enough to share with a family of four (two adults & two children)

>lots of baby spinach
>1 handful lettuce (whatever kind you have on hand)
>½ handful broccoli sprouts
>1 carrot
>1 Tbsp. nuts or seeds
>1-2 Tbsp. Udo's oil (with DHA)
>2 bananas
>1 C frozen fruit
>water *or* apple juice

Blend until smooth.

Green Chocolate

Thanks for the recipe, Angel!

>2 Tbsp. carob
>10 romaine lettuce leaves
>2 Tbsp. spirulina
>2 bananas
>3 dates
>alfalfa sprouts
>water

Blend and enjoy!

Parsley/Weed/Apple

Thanks for the recipe, Anita S.!

Edible weeds are a great form of natural food and have amazing medicinal properties and create health and vitality. Learn to identify them and know their properties and how to exactly use them.

> 2 handfuls parsley
> 1 handful weeds (more or less, depending on its quality—a nutty tasting one will be better tolerated than a bitter one)
> 1 apple
> 1 C water
> chia seeds.

Blend, then sprinkle with some chia seeds and enjoy!

Morning Mojito

Thanks for the recipe, Annie S.!

Yum! I love adding mint to other smoothies too. So great!

> 1 banana or peach
> 1 apple
> 3-4 large kale leaves
> a few mint leaves
> 1+ C of water
> 4 ice cubes

Blend until smooth.

Favorite Combo

Thanks for the recipe, Annie S.!

We've been doing green smoothies for about four years and my two little boys rarely get sick. When they do, they tell me they'd better eat only fruits and vegetable and smoothies until they are well.

Serves 3-4

1-2 bananas
1 orange
2-3+ large kale leaves (without the large stem)
2-3+ large Swiss chard leaves (without the stem)
1 C frozen strawberries or blueberries
1½ C water (may need more)
2 Tbsp. ground flax seeds

Blend and enjoy!

Apple Lime Smoothie

Thanks for the recipe, Betsy M.!

Serves 1-2

5 medium bananas
2 apples (tart/sweet), cored
2 kale leaves
1 C spinach
juice of 2 medium limes
¼ C water
ice cubes

Blend for one minute and enjoy!

Feel Better Soon Green Smoothie

Thanks for the recipe, Beth W.!

Mix and match fruit, depending on what you have on hand and what is on sale that week. Cantaloupe is good in this smoothie. Pineapple, mango, and bananas make a good tropical smoothie.

1-1½ bunches spinach
any other greens on hand (chard, arugula, kale, lettuce, etc.)
1 celery stalk
1 carrot
1 apple
¼ of a pineapple
2 bananas
1 handful strawberries
2 Tbsp. flaxseed oil
1 baby Thai coconut (meat and water)
1-2 C water
½ tsp. ground ginger root
1 tsp. kelp

Blend all ingredients together!

Tip: Quarter your fresh pineapple and then use one quarter each time.

Everyday Green Smoothie

Thanks for the recipe, Betty D.!

1 C orange juice
1 handful spinach
2 Tbsp. bee pollen
2 C frozen blueberries
optional: ½ C homemade yogurt

Add all ingredients and blend.

Bumble Berry Pie
Thanks for the recipe, Bonnie Z.!

¾ C water
1 handful cut-up rhubarb
1 handful raspberries
1 handful blueberries
½ apple
½ pear
1 big handful spinach, lettuce, or (my favorite) red Swiss chard
bit of maple syrup (your favorite sweetener) for sweetening

Blend and enjoy!

Great Bambino Smoothie
Thanks for the recipe, Brynna H.!

2 C reverse osmosis water
3 large handfuls spinach leaves
2 large collard green leaves (each one about the size of your face)
2 red chard leaves
2 kale leaves
2 Tbsp. flaxseed oil
1 tsp. vanilla
1 Tbsp. raw agave nectar
1 banana
6-8 large frozen strawberries
1 C frozen blueberries
1 large apple or pear, sliced with peel

Blend 2 handfuls spinach with the water. Then add and blend the collards, chard, kale, flaxseed oil, vanilla, and agave. Finally, add the last handful spinach and all the fruit and blend very well. Then serve with a straw and a smile!

Tropical Princess

Thanks for the recipe, Carlin M.!

½ head romaine lettuce
1 C pineapple
1 mango
1-2 bananas
1" piece ginger

Blend and enjoy!

Mateo's Messy Green Smoothie

Thanks for the recipe, Carol B.!

2 C coconut water
1 handful purslane or spinach
1 Tbsp. coconut oil
1 Tbsp. maca
1 Tbsp. chia seeds, soaked for 15-20 min.
1 orange
1 apple
1 banana
1 handful strawberries (leave the tops on)

Blend it up and enjoy!

Anti-Depressant Peach-Banana Smoothie

Thanks for the recipe, Carolyn N.!

1½ C pure or alkaline water
¼ C agave nectar
¼ C aloe vera juice
approx. 1 lb. greens of your choice
1 handful cut-up carrots
1 tsp. bee pollen
1 tsp. maca
3 tsp. VitaMineral Green
4 ripe white peaches (from Costco in the summer) or 1 lb. bag frozen peaches
3 bananas
optional: agave or other sweetener

Blend first eight ingredients together. Then add fruit and optional sweetener and blend until smooth.

Wake-Up Smoothie

Thanks for the recipe, Carry B.!

1 C low-fat organic milk
1 organic banana
2 organic apples
2-3 C organic spinach
1 C frozen blueberries or blackberries
organic flax seeds
honey
organic coconut oil

Blend and enjoy!

Post-Run Smoothie

Thanks for the recipe, Charissa F.!

I run a bit and I want to fuel my body with hydrating, healing nutrition afterward. So this is what I whipped up (based on Tim the Raw Runner's smoothie).

    1 banana
    1 C blueberries
    1 tsp. organic, raw maca
    1 tsp. blue manna flakes (helps adrenals recover)
    1 pinch dulse
    1 Tbsp. North Coast Organic Hemp Protein Powder
    1 Tbsp. raw, organic pumpkin seeds
    spinach (as much as you can fit in your high-speed blender)
    3 ice cubes and some water, as needed to blend

Blend, blend, and blend. It is absolutely delish! (My blog: www.rawroyalty.blogspot.com)

Green Beauty Cilantro Shake

Thanks for the recipe, Charissa F.!

I love this one, because it tastes so different and so refreshing—and it has so many healing minerals and nutrients that help make you look and feel beautiful.

    1 bunch cilantro
    ½ grapefruit (without pith)
    ½ navel orange (with pith)
    ½ C pineapple
    1 Tbsp. honey (to taste)
    1 tsp. blue-green algae flakes
    water, as needed to blend

Blend those greens into submission and enjoy! (My blog: www.rawroyalty.blogspot.com)

Muscle Drink Mix
Thanks for the recipe, Chelsea S.!

Anyone seen "Iron Man"? I was pumped when I saw him drinking a green smoothie! Talk about big muscles!

2 C water
3 Tbsp. flaxseed oil
1-2 Tbsp. psyllium *or* some fiber powder
3 big handfuls spinach
1 handful chard
2-3 kale leaves, stems removed
1-2 apples of your choice (we use Fuji, Braeburn, or Granny Smith)
1-2 bananas, frozen
2 spears fresh pineapple, frozen

Blend and enjoy!

Tropical Dream
Thanks for the recipe, Cheri J.!

My 4-year-old nephew was sick and refused his favorite cooked foods, asking instead for a green smoothie.

3 C almond milk
3 very ripe bananas
1 Tbsp. vanilla
¼ C agave
1 C papaya
1 C pineapple
1 C frozen strawberries
1 C mango
2 C spinach

Blend and enjoy!

Ogre's Blood

Thanks for the recipe, Cheryl M.!

> 1 large handful frozen strawberries
> 1 handful frozen pineapple
> 1 banana
> 2-3 large handfuls spinach
> water

Blend and enjoy!

> *Tip:* I freeze the bags of fresh spinach.

Apple Medley

Thanks for the recipe, Christine! *Ok*

> 1 banana, frozen or fresh
> 1 apple
> ½ C blueberries or other berries (frozen or fresh)
> 3 handfuls spinach
> 1 C water (or to desired consistency) *almond milk*

Blend until smooth. Enjoy!

Best Way to Start the Day Smoothie

Thanks for the recipe, Cindy C.!

I don't do really well with the smoothies that have more greens, so I choose to put more fruit in mine and it seems to agree better with me—although I do try to add more greens all of the time.

1 bunch kale
spinach leaves
2 carrots
2 celery stalks
2 frozen bananas
1 C frozen pineapple chunks
1 C ice
1½ C any nut or seed milk, vanilla flavored
¼ C almonds
¼ C vanilla yogurt
fresh spearmint leaves
stevia or other sweetener (to taste)
flaxseed oil
distilled water

Blend well and enjoy!

> *Tip:* Sometimes I'll substitute peanut butter (homemade) for the almonds. In season, I also may add strawberries or raspberries.

4-3-2-1 Juice

Thanks for the recipe, Cissy!

4 kale leaves, roughly chopped
⅓ bunch parsley
2 celery ribs, roughly chopped
1 apple, chopped
juice of ½ lemon
2 C water (or more, if needed for desired consistency)
optional: 2 tsp. agave nectar (use if apple isn't very sweet)

Blend and enjoy!

Zesty Green Smoothie

Thanks for the recipe, Colleen!

I got the original idea from Dr. Oz on "Oprah," but have tailored it to taste the way I like it.

> 1 very large handful of one of the following greens: spinach, kale, green, red or white chard
> small bit of parsley
> 1 celery stick
> 1 Granny Smith apple
> 1 small piece of ginger
> 4 Tbsp. fresh lemon or lime juice
> 24 oz. water

Blend and enjoy! This smoothie also works great frozen if you need to take it with you the next day.

Green Goddess Smoothie

Thanks for the recipe, Connie B.!

I came up with this smoothie recipe when my husband decided he wanted to take smoothies to work and drink them throughout the day. I make it almost every morning, and he never gets tired of it. Best of all, it makes him feel and look terrific!

> 2-3 C water
> 1 handful soaked almonds
> 1 Tbsp. ground flax seeds or flaxseed oil
> 1 scoop plant-based protein powder (I use Life's Basics Plant Protein)
> 1 Tbsp. coconut oil
> *optional*: ¼ C dates *or* agave nectar (to sweeten)
> 1-1½ C frozen blueberries or other berries
> 2 large Swiss chard leaves
> 2 large kale leaves
> 1 handful spinach leaves
> 1 banana or frozen banana pieces
> *optional*: ice

Put first six ingredients in a high-powered blender and blend well. Add fruit, green leafy veggies, and optional ice, then blend again until smooth. Serve with a straw.

Fruity Delight

Thanks for the recipe, Connie N.!

      spinach
      fruit juice (apple is good, or use water if worried about too much sugar)
      apples
      pineapple
      any other fruit (I love strawberries)
      optional: agave

Blend and enjoy!

Sweetheart Breakfast Smoothie

Thanks for the recipe, Dallas J.

This is the one my sweetheart will drink!

      fresh pineapple
      fresh apple
      fresh spinach
      2 Tbsp. golden flax seeds
      2 fresh stevia leaves
      2 Tbsp. fresh coconut *or* 1 Tbsp. coconut oil
      water
      ice

Blend and enjoy!

Dan's Superfood Powerhouse
Thanks for the recipe, by Dan G.!

Makes about 40 oz.

1 apple
1 banana
1 C berries (blueberries, raspberries, blackberries, and/or strawberries)
2 Tbsp. raw cacao nibs or powder
approx. ¼ C goji berries
approx. ¼ C soaked chia seeds
1" piece yellow ginger
1 celery stalk
small handful parsley
2 large handfuls spinach or any other leafy green (romaine, mixed greens, kale, etc.)
1 pinch dulse seaweed
2 C water

Blend ingredients together well.

Dandy of a Smoothie
Thanks for the recipe, by Dana E.!

baby spinach or any other green
dandelion leaves from the garden
parsley
bananas
frozen peaches and mangos
1 pint blueberries
1 dollop organic olive oil with antioxidants
optional: 1 small (or ½ large) avocado

Blend and enjoy!

Dave's Fave

Thanks for the recipe, Dave S.!

Beautiful jade green, smooth, delicious, and impossibly nutritious.

> 1 apple
> 1 celery stalk
> 10-12 pieces parsley
> 1 big handful spinach
> 1 large carrot (or 2 small ones)
> ginger root, about the size of your thumb
> approx. ⅓ cucumber
> 1 avocado
> 1 glug zero-fat yogurt
> 2 glugs apple cider

Wash and core the apple, rinse the veggies, peel the ginger root, coarsely chop the celery, apple, carrots and cucumber, heave everything into the BlendTec, hit the whole food smoothie button and it's ready in 50 seconds. Enjoy!

Ginger's Garden Goodness

Thanks for the recipe, David J.!

> blender full of kale
> 1 handful parsley
> 2½ C water
> 1 large grapefruit, peeled
> 1 mango
> a few frozen strawberries

Blend the first three ingredients for 90 seconds. Add the fruit and blend another 90 seconds. Enjoy!

The Umbrella

Thanks for the recipe, David S.!

I call it "The Umbrella" because it offers basic coverage!

> 1 carrot
> 1 celery stalk
> 1 banana
> 1 Roma tomato
> 1 Granny Smith apple
> 3 handfuls spinach
> 1 C water
> 1 C ice cubes
> ½ C berries (strawberries, blueberries, raspberries, whatever…)

Blend and enjoy!

Savory V-8

Thanks for the recipe, Debbie W.!

My favorite green smoothie right now is all veggies because after 2 years, I am tired of sweet green smoothies. I like to eat my fruit and drink my veggies!

> 2 C alkaline water
> 1 big kale leaf
> 2 big handfuls spinach or other greens
> 1 regular carrot
> 2 or so tomatoes *or* a couple tablespoons tomato paste
> approx. ¼ onion *or* 1 handful green onions (for less onion flavor)
> 2 celery stalks
> ½ - ⅓ English cucumber and/or zucchini
> 1 Tbsp. flax seeds
> basil leaves, cilantro, or any herb that sounds good (to taste)
> 1 tsp. sole
> juice of 1-2 lemons
> *optional*: red pepper (for spice)

Blend and enjoy!

Fungus the Bogey Man Juice

Thanks for the recipe, Debra!

      1 handful spinach
      frozen mango
      frozen pineapple chunks
      frozen pear
      mint
      filtered water

Blend and enjoy!

Coconut Smoothie

Thanks for the recipe, Della M.!

      1 young Thai coconut (water and nut meat)
      1 Tbsp. raw tahini
      1-2 C spinach
      1 Tbsp. carob powder
      optional: bee pollen and/or maca root

Blend and enjoy!

Blue-Green Smoothie

Thanks for the recipe, Denis!

      banana
      strawberries
      blueberries
      kale (spinach when kale is not available)
      water (or sometimes orange juice, to change the taste a bit)
      ground flax seeds

Blend and enjoy!

WOW! It's Green

Thanks for the recipe, Devan H.!

> 1 C water
> 1 mango
> 1 overripe pear
> ¼ C pineapple
> handfuls and handfuls of spinach

Blend well, and even your 12-year-old who's convinced she doesn't like some fruits will slurp it up!

Front Lawn

Thanks for the recipe, Diana W.!

I have come to LOVE this combination and don't find myself varying from it much.

Makes 4 cups

> 1 C filtered water or coconut water
> ½ - ¾ lb. organic baby spinach (½ - ¾ box found at Costco)
> 2-3 kale leaves (stems removed), 2 chard leaves and stems, or some of each
> ½" slice organic lemon (peel, pith, and all)
> 1 ripe banana
> 1 large handful strawberries (about 6 large ones)
> 1½ C frozen blueberries
> flaxseed oil
> *optional*: ½ avocado

Blend and enjoy!

> *Tip:* I've also varied this by omitting the lemon and avocado, instead adding a big spoonful of coconut meat (found in a jar at the health food store) or even coconut milk. Really yummy, but a bit heavier.

Persimmon-Pear Delight

Thanks for the recipe, Dina S.!

> 2 C cold water
> 5 chard leaves
> 2 pears, in chunks
> 1 persimmon
> 2 dates

Blend and enjoy!

Strawberry-Banana Bliss

Thanks for the recipe, Dina S.!

> juice of 2 oranges
> enough water to bring the juice up to 2 C
> 1 bunch spinach (about 2 C)
> 1 frozen banana
> 1-2 C strawberries (can be frozen)
> 2 dates

Blend and enjoy!

Mad For Mango

Thanks for the recipe, Dina S.!

> 2 C water
> 1 large mango, peeled and pitted
> 1 C parsley
> 1 frozen banana
> 1 handful goji berries or raisins

Blend and enjoy!

Green Lemonade
Thanks for the recipe, Elizabeth B.!

> juice of ½ lemon (approx. ⅛ C)
> 1 peach
> 1-2 handfuls of red grapes
> spinach
> ¾ - 1 C water

Blend and enjoy!

Ruby-Green Twist
Thanks for the recipe, Elizabeth B.!

> 2 grapefruits
> ½ - 1 bunch cilantro
> water

Blend and enjoy!

Pineapple Mango Julep
Thanks for the recipe, Ellen M.!

> 1 big bunch spinach or spring mix
> ½ bunch fresh mint
> 1 Tbsp. coconut oil *or* ½ avocado
> 1 fresh or frozen banana
> fresh or frozen pineapple
> fresh or frozen mango
> fresh or frozen strawberries

Blend until smooth.

Green Smoothie Smorgasbord Delight

Thanks for the recipe, Esther H.!

> 1 handful spinach (always my base)
> approx. 2 C water
> 3 baby carrots plus 1 top
> fresh peppermint leaves from 1 stem
> ½ avocado
> 1 small banana
> ¼ C blueberries
> 3 apricots
> 2 Tbsp. agave
> water, to desired consistency
> *optional*: few shakes of cinnamon

Note: You could add 1 Tbsp. each brown and gold flax seeds and brown sesame seeds. I also like to add ground pumpkin and sunflower seeds. When I have beet greens and Swiss chard, I add a leaf of those. When the marshmallow, "mouse ear," and Lambs Quarter come, I add a few. Experiment for best taste!

Blend and enjoy!

Cilantro-Pineapple Smoothie

Thanks for the recipe, Evelyn B.!

> 2 cucumbers, peeled and chopped
> ½ pineapple, peeled and chopped
> 1 large bunch cilantro
> ½ C coconut water or filtered water
> 2 Tbsp. (or more, to taste) stevia
> 2 tsp. vanilla extract

Blend all ingredients until smooth.

Chocolate Morning Delight
Thanks for the recipe, Evi!

> 4 oz. frozen blueberries
> 4 oz. frozen cherries
> ½ ripe banana *or* ½ avocado (if you don't like bananas)
> 2 Tbsp. flax seeds
> 2 Tbsp. maple syrup
> 1+ C water
> ⅛ C cocoa (the HFS kind without sugar or additives)
> 1 tsp. vanilla
> 4 C baby greens, frozen greens, or other dark green lettuce
> 1 C cabbage (cut into chunks)

Combine water with banana (or avocado), flax seeds, maple syrup, cocoa, and vanilla in a high-powered blender. Blend until the flax seeds are ground and mixture is smooth and thick. Add cabbage and greens and blend, adding more water as needed. Add frozen berries and blend until smooth. Enjoy!

Tatiana's Traffic Light Smoothie
Thanks for the recipe, Evi!

My 5-year-old daughter Tatiana loves this smoothie with a big straw!

Red Light
> 1 handful frozen raspberries, strawberries, or cherries (mix if you like)
> ½ red beet

Yellow Light
> ½ mango
> 1 handful frozen pineapple

Green Light
> 2 kiwis
> 1 handful frozen spinach and/or kale
> *optional*: thick coconut milk mixed with some vanilla

Blend each of the "lights" separately. First mix the green light and pour into large glass. Then mix the yellow light and pour on top of the green. Lastly, mix the red light and pour on the top. Sometimes I add the optional coconut milk in between the lights for more flavor and smoothness.

Green Oats Smoothie

Thanks for the recipe, Evi!

½ C rolled oats, soaked in water overnight
½ avocado
1 handful mixed greens
1 C almond, rice, or any nut or seed milk
1 Tbsp. flaxseed oil
1 tsp. vanilla
water, as needed

Blend everything together and enjoy getting a healthy portion of oats in your smoothie!

Christmas Morning Smoothie

Thanks for the recipe, Fiona B.!

It was Christmas, two years ago, and I was determined to keep a healthy diet through the holidays without feeling deprived. I made a list of festive ingredients and created the following.

1 C water or coconut water
1 C fresh organic cranberries
1 good-sized apple (or 2 smaller ones)
spinach (as much or as little as you'd typically put in your drink)
raw honey (local, if possible), to taste
cinnamon, to taste

Blend and enjoy!

Raw Green Smoothie

Thanks for the recipe, Frankie M.!

2 C green grapes
2 oranges, washed and peeled with veggie peeler to retain pith
1 Bartlett pear
2 bananas, fresh or frozen
2 C kale or spinach
1 C water
4 C ice

Blend and enjoy!

Green Giant Smoothie

Thanks for the recipe, Frankie M.!

> 1½ C coconut water
> 4 C spinach
> 1 C kale
> 1 banana
> 1 tsp. spirulina
> honey (to taste)
> *optional*: 1 small knob ginger

Blend and enjoy!

Winter Wellness Soup/Smoothie

Thanks for the recipe, Frankie M.!

> 1 parsnip, unpeeled
> 1 big handful spinach
> 1 large clove garlic
> ½" piece ginger root, peeled
> ⅓ cucumber, unpeeled
> 2 Tbsp. apple cider vinegar
> 1 Tbsp. raw honey (local, if possible)
> ¼ tsp. salt
> 2 dashes hot pepper flakes
> 1 dash cayenne
> 1 handful pine nuts
> water

Blend very well. Enjoy as a thick smoothie or a soup, depending on how much water you add.

Montel Williams' Green Smoothie

Thanks for the recipe, Frankie M.!

> 2 bananas
> 3 oranges, washed and peeled with veggie peeler to retain pith
> 1 head romaine lettuce
> 4 C water/ice

Blend and enjoy!

Cherry Bomb Smoothie

Thanks for the recipe, Glenna P.!

We've discovered that cherries make a wonderful addition to our morning smoothies. We prefer ours more watery, like juice, but the addition of ice would make this recipe more like a traditional smoothie. The kids love this one because it's tarty-sweet.

1½ C pitted red cherries
1½ C frozen or fresh blueberries
1½ C filtered water
4 C organic baby spinach
3 Tbsp. flaxseed oil
ice as desired
optional: 1 squirt of local honey

Add all ingredients to blender. Blend, blend, blend...pour...enjoy!

Easy Green Smoothie

Thanks for the recipe, Gord!

Make your regular favorite fruit smoothie, then add a handful of spinach or other good greens. Blend and enjoy!

Chocolate Oatmeal Smoothie

Thanks for the recipe, Greg M.!

½ C oatmeal
8 oz. water
3 Tbsp. chocolate protein powder
1 large handful spinach
1 sliced apple
1 sliced banana
2 Tbsp. flax seeds

Blend and enjoy!

Sweet Smoothie

Thanks for the recipe, Guy!

I started with all fruit and 10% greens—now I try to get in close to 50% greens. I also add 1 celery stalk for the organic sodium, which has cured my heartburn.

serving of grapes
blueberries
2 oranges
banana, frozen
organic baby spinach, packed into the blender container
peach segments, frozen
sweet dates *or* stevia

Blend and enjoy!

Bok Choy Cooler

Thanks for the recipe, Hannah M.!

1-2 C bok choy
1 whole English cucumber
10 parsley, basil, or mint leaves
1 tsp. spirulina
1 tsp. maca
2 pears
1 apple
1"-2" piece fresh ginger
2 C or more water (depending how thick or thin you like it)
optional: Sometimes I add more fruit.

Blend and enjoy!

Fruity Energy Smoothie

Thanks for the recipe, Hannah M.!

       any greens you like
       1 banana
       2 apples
       1 tsp. mesquite
       1 Tbsp. maca
       water to cover

Blend and enjoy!

Tropical Tummy Soother

Thanks for the recipe, Heather H.!

Pregnant with my fourth child, there are just some things that I can't stomach. However, this green smoothie is my Tropical Tummy Soother, with flax and kefir to aid my digestive system, pineapple for the bromelain, and ginger to calm my stomach on those icky days. Plus, it's 12 servings of fruits and veggies if I can't get anything else down!

       3 C spinach/chard mix
       2 oranges
       2 bananas
       1"-2" section pineapple (core included)
       1 C papaya *or* 2 peaches
       1 C strawberries
       1 Tbsp. flax seeds
       ¼ C plain kefir
       1"-2" piece fresh ginger
       optional: 1 C water (if needed)

Blend a minute or so, then enjoy! Hope you like it— it's getting me through this early pregnancy.

Almost Green & Happy

Thanks for the recipe, Heidi B.!

spinach (enough to fill blender)
organic spring greens (from Costco)
chard
1 pear
1 handful grapes
2 tsp. organic coconut oil
1 C frozen berries (from Costco)

Blend and enjoy!

Green Shake

Thanks for the recipe, Helen V.!

plain milk kefir (homemade)
bananas
peaches (frozen)
pineapple (frozen)
spinach (raw)
coconut oil
hemp seeds

Blend and enjoy!

Green Smoothie

Thanks for the recipe, JC!

> 2 C water
> ½ batch kale (about 6 leaves with stems)
> 1 Tbsp. flaxseed oil
> ¼ lemon (peel and seeds included)
> 12 ice cubes
> ½ batch spinach (about ½ lb.)
> 1 banana
> 1 C frozen mango
> *optional*: ¼ C frozen cranberries or frozen triple berries
> *optional*: ⅓ lb. soft tofu (to make creamy)

Blend the first five ingredients. Then add the remaining ingredients and blend again. Enjoy!

Pineapple Delight

Thanks for the recipe, Jada D.!

> 1 cucumber
> 1 lime, peeled
> ½ - 1 C pineapple
> cilantro (to taste)
> 1 tsp. spirulina
> 1 pinch sea salt
> 1 pinch cinnamon
> *optional*: agave *or* stevia

Blend and enjoy!

The "Beet"le Juice

Thanks for the recipe, Jason C.!

    1 red beet, peeled and diced
    2 C spinach
    1 date
    1 apple, chunked
    ice and water (to achieve desired consistency)

Blend and enjoy!

Cancun Green

Thanks for the recipe, Jeanne!

Several years ago we were staying at the Gran Melia in Cancun, Mexico. We ate at the breakfast buffet in the hotel almost every morning because the food was so good. One of the beverages was a drink that was green in color. My husband tried it, on the recommendation that it was very good. He got hooked on it, as did I. I looked at the ingredients on the dispenser, and then when we came home, I experimented with the amounts until I came up with what was similar and a flavor we liked.

Book: Jeanne's Recipes
Chapter: Beverages

Makes 6-8 servings

    2-4 ribs celery
    4-6 stems fresh parsley
    2-4 C packed or 2-4 handfuls fresh spinach
    6 C orange juice (1 12-oz. can frozen, reconstituted)

Adjust amount of ingredients to desired taste. Blend ingredients well. Refrigerate. Enjoy this healthful, refreshing beverage.

Nanacolada

Thanks for the recipe, Jeannette C.!

I came up with this one after my last trip to Hawaii and could not find good organic pineapples locally.

Makes 1 16-oz. serving

1 medium organic banana
2 Tbsp. pineapple juice concentrate
¼ C raw, unsweetened coconut
1-1½ C ice
6 oz. water
2 C spinach

Blend all ingredients.

Green Refresher

Thanks for the recipe, Jeff N.!

OK

2 ripe peaches *nectarines*
1 C of pineapple *1 cup pineapple*
1 handful kale *1 cup packed greens*
little bit of water *½ cup water*
3 ice cubes *3 ice cubes*

Put all ingredients in your high-powered blender and blend until completely smooth.

Kid's Berry Smoothie

Thanks for the recipe, Jen H.!

Makes 6 servings

2 C water
2 C baby spinach
2 Tbsp. refrigerated flaxseed oil
⅓ C light agave
2 medium bananas, frozen
1 C strawberries, frozen
1 C three-berry mix, frozen (blueberries, raspberries, blackberries, or marionberries)

I run my BlendTec first on the "Milkshake" setting and then on the "Whole Juice" setting.

Note: According to Fitday.com, this is 99 calories per serving.

Strawberry Lemonade Green Smoothie

Thanks for the recipe, Jenni C.!

The chia gel gives a smooth consistency without adding banana.

10 frozen strawberries
⅛ - ¼ whole lemon with peel *or* ½ whole lemon without peel
2 large handfuls spinach or other greens
1 Tbsp. agave nectar
¼ C chia gel (made by soaking ⅓ C chia seeds in 2 C water)

Blend all ingredients, serve, and enjoy!

Hawaiian Delight

Thanks for the recipe, Jenni C.!

This particular smoothie I got very little of because my girls liked it so much they kept asking for more.

>lots of spinach or any mixture of greens
>½ pear
>1 banana
>1 ring pineapple
>1 C water
>1 C coconut milk (I prefer Thai Kitchen brand)
>1-2 Tbsp. flax seeds
>*optional*: coconut oil

Combine all ingredients and blend until smooth.

Cranberry Orange Green Smoothie

Thanks for the recipe, Jenni C.!

This is sweet and tangy! Great around Thanksgiving!

>1 kale stalk
>2 huge handfuls spinach
>1 handful fresh cranberries
>2 oranges
>½ banana
>*optional*: stevia *or* agave nectar (to taste)

Blend and enjoy!

Shrek Shake

Thanks for the recipe, Jennifer H.!

> 1-2 Tbsp. flax seeds
> 1-2 bananas (ripe)
> 2 handfuls frozen strawberries
> 1 scoop protein powder
> 1½-2 C spinach
> 3-4 large kale leaves
> 3-4 collard green leaves
> *optional*: 4 ice cubes (to make cold)

Blend the flax seeds to break down. Add the bananas, strawberries, and protein powder and blend well. Then add each green type one at a time, blending after each addition. Add the optional ice and blend very well. Enjoy!

Mango 'Moothie

Thanks for the recipe, Jennifer R.!

It makes a bright green, lovely smoothie. My son runs around the house screaming "'Moothie, please! 'Moothie, please!"

> 1 C water
> spinach and a little kale to make 3 C blended
> 1 spoonful coconut oil (it makes it sooo creamy and smooth!)
> 1-2 C frozen mangos or peaches

Blend until smooth and enjoy!

The Ultimate Kid-Friendly Smoothie

Thanks for the recipe, Jennifer S.!

This is one of our "starter" ones that I've even stirred into my baby's oatmeal.

> 2 C spinach
> 1 frozen banana
> 1 C frozen grapes
> 1 C water
> 1 C ice cubes

Blend according to blender instructions. Pour into clear glasses and enjoy!

Classic Green Smoothie

Thanks for the recipe, Jennifer S.!

    1 handful kale leaves
    1 handful beet greens
    1 Tbsp. flaxseed oil
    1 Tbsp. aloe vera juice
    1 banana
    1 handful any favorite fruit (kiwi, mango, etc.)

Blend your greens with water until smooth. Add the rest to the blender and mix until smooth. Enjoy!

Every Morning Smoothie

Thanks for the recipe, Jenny W.!

    1 Tbsp. golden flax seeds
    1 tsp. Brewer's Yeast
    1 pinch green tea leaves
    1 pinch açaí powder (Nutiva Naturals)
    several handfuls kale or chard
    1 C unsweetened chocolate almond milk
    stevia (to taste)
    1 scoop Brendan Brazier's Whole Food Health Optimizer (chocolate)
    ½ C berry blend (from Trader Joe's)
    approx. 2 C ice (for thick, eat-with-a-spoon consistency)

Blend the first seven ingredients until smooth. Then add the last three ingredients and blend again.

Jenner Mix

Thanks for the recipe, Jenny W.!

This one is simply my afternoon pick-me-up smoothie.

> 1 C water
> 2 C spinach
> approx. ¼ banana
> stevia (to taste)
> approx. 1 C ice

Blend until smooth.

Frogs in a Blender

Thanks for the recipe, Jessica L.!

> 1 banana
> 6-7 frozen strawberries
> 1 C rice milk
> 1-2 C water (based on desired consistency)
> 2 HUGE handfuls organic baby spinach leaves

Blend till smooth. Enjoy!

EB Cherry Green Smoothie

Thanks for the recipe, Jo M.!

> ½ C spinach
> ½ C beet greens
> 2 Tbsp. flaxseed oil
> stevia (to taste)
> 2 C water
> 2 frozen bananas
> frozen bing cherries, pitted (to taste)

Blend until smooth.

Cantaloupe Green Smoothie

Thanks for the recipe, Jo M.!

    2 C water
    ½ C spinach
    ½ C collard greens
    2 Tbsp. flaxseed oil
    stevia (to taste)
    2 frozen bananas
    ½ large cantaloupe or 1 whole small cantaloupe (rind removed)
    2 C water

Blend until smooth.

Pineapple Coconut Smoothie

Thanks for the recipe, Jo M.!

    collard greens and spinach
    stevia
    flaxseed oil
    coconut water
    frozen bananas
    pineapple spears
    frozen apricots

Blend until smooth.

Creamy Mango Delight
Thanks for the recipe, Joe!

This is one of my all-time favorites. It's creamy and has a hint of chocolate—plus, who doesn't love mangos?

Makes 64 oz.

2 C filtered water
½ bunch romaine lettuce
2 C mango
1 C pineapple
1 large banana
½ avocado
2 Tbsp. raw cocoa
2 Tbsp. raw flax seeds
1 Tbsp. raw bee pollen

Blend and enjoy!

Family Morning Smoothie

Thanks for the recipe, Julie M.!

We have two boys, 13 and 17. They fight over the fullest glass, even if it's just by a smidgen! And our granddaughters love to drink this from their "sippie cups"—minus the nuts and flaked coconut, of course!

approx. 2 C different greens (see below)

2 C alkaline water

2 Tbsp. flaxseed oil

¼ can unsweetened coconut milk *or* ¼ C of fresh coconut water from a baby Thai coconut

4 frozen strawberries (may use any other berry or a mixture)

2 frozen bananas

raw agave nectar (to taste)

optional:1 C almond milk made from raw almonds is extra wonderful!

optional: ½ avocado

optional: fresh or flaked unsweetened coconut

optional: 5 pecans or almonds

Pulse blend the greens and water until liquefied. Then add the remaining ingredients and pulse blend until smooth. Blend for approx. 10 seconds, then turn on high for another 20 seconds.

Note: Mild tasting greens I've had success with:
> beet greens
> chard
> spinach
> dandelion greens

The following greens are good, especially kale, but I use them sparingly for my boys because they don't like a strong "green-tasting" smoothie:
> kale
> collard greens

Guess What! Smoothie

Thanks for the recipe, Karen!

>   3 types of greens including spinach
>   3 fruits including banana

Blend until smooth.

Good Morning Smoothie

Thanks for the recipe, Karen!

Just a smoothie that I put together for when I am in a hurry.

>   1 banana
>   1 helping vegan protein powder
>   1 Tbsp. flax seeds
>   1 tsp. calcium supplement powder
>   ½ C blueberries
>   1 Tbsp. almond butter
>   1 handful spinach

Add little water to blend…and YUM!

Purple Smoothie Surprise

Thanks for the recipe, Kathleen C.!

>   *Makes approx. 5 C or enough for 1 adult & 2 smoothie-lovin' kids*

>   1-2 C homemade almond milk (may use less or use water for some of the liquid)
>   2 frozen bananas
>   1-2 C frozen blueberries
>   1 BIG handful spinach
>   5 fresh strawberries
>   fresh coconut water (to taste)

Blend until smooth.

Willa's "More-More" Smoothie!

Thanks for the recipe, Kathryn R.!

    romaine lettuce
    a little water
    bananas
    frozen mixed berries

Blend the romaine and water, then add the fruit and blend again.

Baby Pleaser

Thanks for the recipe, Kathy K.!

My daughter loves this recipe, and when she babysat, she made this smoothie for a 1-year-old who loved it and shrieked when she thought she wasn't getting anymore.

    ½ - 1 lb. spinach
    1 banana
    2 apples
    1 handful blueberries
    5-10 frozen strawberries
    optional: 1 tsp. coconut oil
    optional: 1-3 Tbsp. hemp protein

Blend and enjoy!

Kathy's Supertastic Green Smoothie

Thanks for the recipe, Kathy R.!

> 1 C coconut water
> 1 ripe banana
> 1 C frozen strawberries (from Costco)
> 8 oz. fresh, organic, baby spinach (from Costco)
> 2 large kale leaves (organic)
> 1 C Swiss chard leaf or collard greens
> 1 heaping Tbsp. flax seeds (milled, organic)

Put coconut water, banana, and strawberries into BlendTec (or other high-powered blender). Blend on "Whole Juice" for one cycle. Add spinach and blend on "Whole Juice" for one cycle, then add kale and blend again on "Whole Juice" for another cycle. Add remaining ingredients and again blend on "Whole Juice" for one cycle.

Pour over ice in a large cup. Put remainder in refrigerator in the blender container.

> *Tip:* When I'm ready for more, I just put the container back on the blender base and give it a little spin on "Speed Up" just in case it started to separate.

Greenie Meanie

Thanks for the recipe, Kathy T.!

> ⅓ bag baby spinach
> ¼ - ½ C plain any nut or seed milk
> 1 banana
> 10 - 20 strawberries
> ½ C blueberries
> ½ C pineapple, peaches, or mango

Blend and enjoy!

Pirate Grog

Thanks for the recipe, Kellie L.!

Named for my 3-year-old son. Now, the baby pirate in the house, who just turned 1 year last week, LOVES our smoothies!

       greens (mostly kale, spinach)
       ½ C water
       ½ C any natural juice
       1 Tbsp. flaxseed oil
       1 Tbsp. almond butter
       1 banana (frozen or fresh)
       ½ C pineapple
       ½ C frozen berries (whatever variety is on hand)

Blend and enjoy!

Peach Pizazz

Thanks for the recipe, Kim H.!

I didn't discover putting ripe peaches into my smoothie until this summer. I really like them a lot and now I'm buying a lot of peaches!

       3½ C water
       ½ lb. fresh spinach
       2 Tbsp. flaxseed oil
       1 very small wedge lemon (peel and all)
       ¼ C agave nectar
       1-2 frozen bananas (depending on creaminess consistency you desire)
       ½ C frozen blueberries
       1-2 small, very ripe peaches

Blend and enjoy!

Nana-Blue Cressie
Thanks for the recipe, Kit B.!

Serves 1 adult

1 C fresh watercress
⅓ - ½ frozen banana
1 C frozen blueberries
1 Tbsp. ground flaxseed
½ - 1 C frozen spinach
1 C water
optional: 1 Brazil nut (I add to get Selenium)

Blend in blender, slowly increasing to high speed for 30 seconds. Add water to thin, if desires.

Dark Secret
Thanks for the recipe, Kristen P.!

1 handful strawberries
1 BIG handful spinach (sometimes I also use some kale leaves)
1 banana
2 handfuls red grapes
1 handful frozen berries (any kind)
optional: 1 small C ice

Blend and enjoy!

PeachANUT Butter Smoothie
Thanks for the recipe, Lala!

spinach and water base with 2 kale leaves
2 bananas
strawberries
lots of frozen peaches (they have to be yummy, flavorful peaches)
1-2 fresh pears
flaxseed oil *or* flax seeds
2 Tbsp. natural peanut butter
optional: dash of stevia

Blend and enjoy!

Jalyn's Good Stuff Smoothie

Thanks for the recipe, Latisha L.!

We've tried several combinations, but this combination is our family favorite. My 4-year-old daughter tasted it on video for the first time and, in her words, "Everyone has to make this, because it has a lot of fruit... and good stuff in it."

Makes 4 tall, tasty servings

2 large turnip green leaves
2 large curly kale leaves
2 large mustard green leaves
1 handful arugula
2 Tbsp. cilantro
2 Tbsp. parsley
¼ C finely ground nuts (macadamias, pecans, almonds, cashew)
½ pineapple with juice (at least ¼ C of juice)
1 mango, sliced or chopped
¼ C strawberries
¼ C blueberries
1½ tsp. agave
1 C coconut water
2 Tbsp. protein powder
2 Tbsp. flax seeds, whole ground
optional: ice, as needed or desired

Blend well and enjoy!

Go-To Smoothie

Thanks for the recipe, Laura S.!

1 C water
⅓ bag baby spinach or equivalent amount chard or beet greens
1 frozen lemon cube (see below)
1 small apple (cored/seeded)
1 C frozen blueberries

Blend and enjoy!

Tip: Once a week I blend an entire lemon with water and pour into ice cube trays.

No-Fruit Green Smoothie

Thanks for the recipe, Laura T.!

If you're diabetic or hypoglycemic, or just trying to reduce sugars in your diet, you may wish to cut fruits and maximize greens. I spent seven years of my adolescence and young adult life in bed with serious health issues. I don't do well with sugar of any kind, and so I devised this green smoothie that is highly alkaline and low in sugar.

> 1 avocado
> 1 large cucumber
> 2 C spinach
> 2 large collard green leaves
> 2 black kale leaves
> juice of 2-3 lemons (to taste)
> 1⅓ C water
> *optional*: a few slices of Gala apples

Combine all in a high-powered blender. Purée well and enjoy.

Kiss Me in the Morning

Thanks for the recipe, Leigh!

This is an addictive afternoon snack that gives you more kick than coffee as well as fresh breath all evening and even the next morning.

> 1 C orange juice (fresh or from frozen concentrate)
> 1 C parsley (curly or flat)
> ½ C frozen mango chunks

Blend and enjoy!

Sydney's Soccer Night Special

Thanks for the recipe, Leigh!

Making it to the soccer field by 5:30 p.m. with homework and dinner complete is not easy. Dinner is often in the car (drive-thru nuggets and fries?). I think we can do better! We blend up Sydney's Soccer Night special in a couple of minutes, put it in a travel cup with a straw, and we are off!

> 1 C chocolate almond milk
> 1 C baby organic spinach
> ¼ avocado
> 1 Tbsp. peanut butter
> ½ C uncooked rolled oats
> ½ C crushed ice
> *optional*: agave (if needed)

Blend and enjoy!

Peachy Keen Green Smoothie

Thanks for the recipe, Linda K.!

> several handfuls kale and spinach (1-to-3 ratio of greens)
> 1 whole peach, pitted
> ½ frozen banana
> 1 handful each fresh raspberries, blueberries, and red grapes
> filtered water or ice (to thin to a drinkable consistency)

Blend and enjoy!

Linda's Morning Wake-up Call
Thanks for the recipe, Linda O.!

Makes 28-30 oz. (about 3-4 servings)

2 C spinach
2 C cucumber
1 head celery
½" piece (or 1 tsp. grated) ginger root
1 bunch parsley
2 apples
juice of 1 lime
juice of ½ lemon
optional: fresh pineapple and banana, if desired

Blend all together well.

Kid-Friendly Green Drink a.k.a. Kenzie's Concoction
Thanks for the recipe, Linda O.!

3-4 handfuls fresh spinach
1 banana
1 C Costco's frozen fruit mix
100% orange juice or orange-combo juice (to taste)
water, to preferred consistency

Stuff fresh spinach (compressing it) into a high-powered blender. Add banana and frozen fruit mix. Then add 100% orange juice or an orange-combo juice (orange-passion fruit or pineapple-orange-banana, etc.)—the amount to add varies depending on how thick you want it. The frozen fruit makes it more like a smoothie. Blend for at least 1½ minutes. Taste to see if it needs anything else, such as more fruit. Enjoy!

Tropical Green Smoothie

Thanks for the recipe, Linda P.!

1 C water (preferably alkaline)
1 handful spinach (or any greens you like in smoothies)
2 Brazil nuts (for selenium)
1 "blurp" of vanilla
1 ripe banana
frozen pineapple chunks to taste (usually I put enough in to raise the level of the blended drink up to 2¼ - 2½ C)

Blend and enjoy!

Tip: Putting the banana and pineapple on top helps "push" the greens into the blender blades. I like mild wild greens in season. Marshmallow is always mild (to me) and is a good addition.

Grapefruit Delight

Thanks for the recipe, Lisa!

¼ pink grapefruit
½ cucumber
1-2 celery stalks
1 banana *or* agave (for sweetness)
1 handful spinach

Blend and enjoy!

James Family Sonic Jolt Smoothie

Thanks for the recipe, Lisa J.!

> spinach (sometimes we use kale)
> water
> juice of some white grapes
> mango (sometimes we use banana)
> pineapple (frozen, if the other fruit is fresh)
> strawberries
> hemp seeds
> dulse flakes

Blend the first three ingredients in a BlendTec on the "Whole Juice" cycle. Then add the remaining ingredients and blend on the "Smoothie" cycle. Enjoy!

Mom's No-Guilt Banana-Nut Smoothie

Thanks for the recipe, Lori M.!

Forget the kids—this is MY favorite healthful "dessert" smoothie!

> 1½ C almond milk (sometimes I include some coconut milk)
> 2 C spinach
> 1 C frozen banana chunks
> 1 Tbsp. peanut butter
> *optional*: 1-2 Tbsp. raw cocoa powder or nibs

Blend and enjoy!

The Frosty Pear

Thanks for the recipe, Lori M.!

Super refreshing on a hot summer day!

> 1 C water
> 1 C frozen pear chunks
> 1 C frozen parsley

Blend and enjoy!

Creamy Mimi

Thanks for the recipe, Mara G.!

> 1-2 C coconut water
> romaine lettuce
> 1 C blueberries
> ½ avocado
> 1 pear
> 1 banana

Blend and enjoy!

Yoda Smoothie

Thanks for the recipe, Marci W.!

> 1 handful spinach
> 2 bananas (the kind with new brown spots are our favorites)
> 4 frozen strawberries (or 4 strawberries and add ice)
> 1 C water
> ½ C plain yogurt *or* kefir

Blend and enjoy!

Basic Green Smoothie

Thanks for the recipe, Marcia!

> ½ C frozen blueberries
> 6 kale leaves or mix of kale with dandelion, collard greens, etc.
> 1 banana
> 1 Tbsp. ground flax seeds
> 1 Tbsp. chlorella powder
> 2 C water

Blend and enjoy!

Nutty & Raw

Thanks for the recipe, Maria S.!

Serves 1 adult

> 1 large ripe banana
> ½ ripe avocado
> ½ apple or pear
> 1 generous handful baby spinach
> 1 small handful raw pecans
> ½ C any nut or seed milk (unsweetened) or any milk
> 1 tsp. ground flax seeds

Blend all ingredients together. Enjoy!

Marsha's Favorite Green Smoothie

Thanks for the recipe, Marsha C.!

> 8 oz. baby spinach leaves
> 1 pineapple
> 1 mango

Blend and enjoy!

Bliss in a BlendTec

Thanks for the recipe, Marti K.!

> ½ avocado
> 1 clove garlic
> lemon peel
> juice of lemon or lime
> 1 handful snap peas
> 1 medium tomato
> 1 medium carrot
> ½ cucumber
> ½ yellow pepper
> ½ bunch cilantro
> ½ head romaine lettuce
> water (enough to make it smooth)
> ice (enough to chill)

Blend and enjoy!

Mulberry Marvel

Thanks for the recipe, Mary M.!

> 1 large banana
> 1 C mulberries (in season in summer)
> 2 C water
> 2 big handfuls romaine lettuce

Blend and enjoy!

Refreshing Peanut Butter Surprise

Thanks for the recipe, Melissa C.!

We love this healthful, refreshing drink. It is a great pick-me-up any time of day.

> 1 large scoop (approx. 3 Tbsp.) natural peanut butter
> 1 large chunk baby spinach
> 1 small handful raisins
> 1 ripe banana
> 1 apple cut into fourths
> 1 large carrot or 4-5 baby carrots
> approx. 1 Tbsp. flax seeds
> favorite yogurt (small container or a few scoops out of a large one)
> 1-2 C fat-free milk
> several scoops ice

Blend in VitaMix or other high-powered blender for about 60 seconds. Taste test and add and modify to suit your taste as you go.

Peanut Butter Smoothie

Thanks for the recipe, Melody!

> frozen fruit (any kind)
> protein powder
> peanut butter
> carrots (usually)
> spinach
> water

> **Note:** If we are having one as a treat, we use the same ingredients but add yogurt and bananas.

Blend and enjoy!

Cool Blue

Thanks for the recipe, Mendy!

> 1 C organic apple juice (add more if needed to thin)
> ½ C frozen peaches
> 1 C frozen blueberries
> 1 C (or more) organic baby spinach
> 1 tsp. raw honey (local, if possible)
> 2 tsp. ground flax seeds

Blend until smooth.

Spirulina Green Smoothie Blast

Thanks for the recipe, Michele C.!

> 1-2 tsp. Hawaiian Spirulina Pacifica
> 2 oz. wheatgrass
> 1-2 tsp. chlorella
> 4-5 kale leaves
> 1 small apple banana
> 1 handful blueberries (fresh or frozen)
> 1 handful strawberries (fresh or frozen)
> 1 carrot
> 1 apple
> ginger (to taste)
> *optional*: ice

Blender in VitaMix or other blender and enjoy!

Chocolate Peanut Butter Green Smoothie

Thanks for the recipe, Michele R.!

> 2-3 bananas
> 1 big bunch greens (spinach, kale, whatever I have)
> 1 Tbsp. natural peanut butter
> 1 Tbsp. agave nectar *or* honey
> 1 C chocolate almond milk
> 2-3 C crushed ice

Blend and enjoy!

Cinnamon Apple Green Smoothie

Thanks for the recipe, Michele R.!

    2-3 bananas
    1 big bunch greens (spinach, kale, etc.)
    1 tsp. cinnamon
    1 C natural apple juice
    2-3 C crushed ice

Blend and enjoy!

Peaches & Green Smoothie

Thanks for the recipe, Michelle H.!

    1 frozen banana
    1 frozen peach
    spinach or chard (enough to fill blender)
    2 tsp. (or more) powdered greens
    juice of 1 small (or ½ large) lemon
    2 C filtered water, chilled
    agave *or* stevia (to taste)

Blend until smooth.

Fruity Green Energy Smoothie

Thanks for the recipe, Minnie!

This fruity green energy smoothie will fill me up for five or more hours and I am not hungry and I have lots of energy.

> 1 apple
> 1 banana
> 1 C strawberries
> ½ C blueberries
> 1 lime
> ¼ beet *or* ½ carrot
> 2 collard green leaves (washed)
> 2 kale leaves (washed)
> 1 handful spinach (washed)
> 1 C water
> 3 tsp. wheat germ
> 1 Tbsp. flaxseed oil
> *optional*: 1 C ice, if the fruit is not frozen
> *optional*: 1 tsp. stevia, if the fruit is not sweet enough

Note: Sometimes I might use other fruit like pineapple and melons or pears—it's up to you.

Blending the fruit in the water first seems to work best in my BlendTec. Enjoy!

Green Smoothie 2

Thanks for the recipe, Monica A.!

1½ C spinach
½ C kale
1 celery stalk
1 carrot
1 pear
1 kiwi
1 peach
½ C mixed frozen berries
2 single-serve packets of stevia
½ C plain yogurt
water filled up to 2 C mark after ingredients are in blender

Blend until smooth.

Carrot Top

Thanks for the recipe, Monika S.!

2 apples, cored and chopped
1 glass water
1 glass apple juice
1 HUGE handful carrot tops, minus the long stems (unless you have a devil of a blender)

Blend well. Carrot tops have a very mild flavor for greens and they are much more nutritious than the root.

Parsley Power

Thanks for the recipe, Monika S.!

OK

2 apples, cored and chopped
1 glass water   1 cup 1/2 instead.
1 glass apple juice
1 HUGE handful fresh parsley   3.4 oz

Blend well. Parsley has a nice, fresh PUNCH.

Moonie's Green Smoothie

Thanks for the recipe, Moon M.!

I drink two 16-oz. glasses of this every day for breakfast.

1 small handful almonds (soaked overnight in water with a dollop of hydrogen peroxide to get rid of fungus)

1 small handful pumpkin and sunflower seeds (soaked the same as the almonds)

1 large glass water

½ frozen banana

2 frozen strawberries

2 slices pear

1 piece of apple (or whatever fruit you like)

1 small piece carrot

1 dollop agave

1 small chunk wheatgrass

1 huge handful spinach

parsley

kale

Swiss chard

In the order given, place ingredients in the BlendTec and press "Whole Juice."

Veggies for Brekkie Smoothie
Thanks for the recipe, Moyne G.!

I'm a big veggie hater, and this is the way I've been able to eat them. Something about the combination of the cucumber and the lime will cover any objectionable flavors.

½ C carrot juice (I am going to try using a whole chunk of carrot one day soon)

½ C raw goat milk kefir

1 lime (rind removed)

1 "chunk" cucumber

¼ avocado

2 handfuls spinach

1 handful any other green (I rotate among collards, kale, chard, dandelion, and red cabbage)

3 Tbsp. raw hemp hearts

2 Tbsp. ground flax seeds

1 Tbsp. flaxseed oil

2 dropperfuls Sweet Leaf liquid stevia

⅔ - ¾ C frozen berries (it's especially yummy with raspberries!)

Blend the first seven ingredients on the BlendTec "Smoothie" setting. Then add the next four ingredients and blend on "Pulse" until smooth. Finally, add the berries and run the "Smoothie" cycle again. Enjoy!

The 2 Roys' and Mom's Green Smoothie
Thanks for the recipe, Nancy!

water (regular temp in winter; cold from being kept in fridge in summer)

greens (we use lettuce, romaine, green leaf, and spinach)

1½-2 bananas

optional: leftover juice from canned fruit (such as pineapple)

optional: VitaMineral greens

Fill water (and optional canned fruit juice, if using) up to line 3 on a BlendTec, then pulse with enough greens so it reaches just over the BlendTec "Home" name. Run on two "Smoothie" cycles, then add the bananas. Run through two more "Smoothie" cycles, adding optional VitaMineral greens during the last cycle if desired.

> **Tip:** If we've bought bananas as a really good deal, we freeze them and pull them out at night for the next morning, or in the morning for that night. You can also put frozen pieces in if you want it really cold, especially for summer.

Green Kiwi Smoothie

Thanks for the recipe, Nancy E.!

several kale stalks
½ celery stalk
2 kiwi
1 banana
1 C distilled water

Blend until smooth.

Grandma's Green Goo

Thanks for the recipe, Nancy G.!

2 C cold water
8+ C fresh spinach
4 frozen strawberries
1 banana *or* avocado
2 tsp. flaxseed oil
2 Tbap.fresh lemon juice
1 tsp. stevia

Blend together until smooth.

Greenhouse, Full Throttle Smoothie

Thanks for the recipe, Nancy N.!

One of my favorite cucumber varieties for growing in my Alaskan greenhouse is called "Sweet Success" and it makes some of the largest, best-tasting cucumbers. Out of resourcefulness and love of cucumbers, I have found that they make a lovely tasting green smoothie. It is so full of that fresh summer pizzazz—the cucumber makes you feel refreshed and relaxed.

Do the following in the order given:

1. Pour 1½ C good water (I use our well water) into your BlendTec blender.
2. Add ¾ - 1 lb. washed, chunked-up, stray vegetables out of the greenhouse (or garden or fridge or pantry)—green tomatoes, yellow squash, green beans, zucchini, bok choy, kale, chard, lettuce, a little sweet basil, etc. The goal is to use up what you have and not waste any of this precious produce. Purée these vegetables for about 30 to 60 seconds or until well broken down.
3. Add 1-3 very large, washed, chunked-up cucumbers, with skin and seeds intact (about 1½-2 lbs.). Purée for about 30 seconds. Watch this for volume as there is a lot of moisture in cucumbers. (I plan on freezing some of my cucumbers this year to see if I can do the same smoothie during the winter).
4. Add 1-2 frozen or fresh bananas and purée until well blended.
5. Add 1-2 medium apples, washed and quartered, with only the flower and stem ends cut away (use any apple other than Red Delicious). Purée until well blended.
6. Taste for sweetness. If more sweetness is desired, add 1-2 Tbsp. raw agave or grade B maple syrup (my taste buds prefer these to stevia or sugar).
7. Blend everything one more time, just until the sweetener is mixed throughout the smoothie.
8. Serve with a green straw and a pansy blossom floating on top (may use edible flower blossom of choice).

Post-Workout Smoothie

Thanks for the recipe, Nick!

8 oz. water

1 banana

1 large handful spinach

1 scoop chocolate protein powder

1 heaping tsp. peanut butter

2 ice cubes

Blend and enjoy!

Post-Workout Green Smoothie

Thanks for the recipe, Nicole M.!

I came up with this recipe as a post-weight workout meal. The coconut water is great because it has electrolytes, and the hemp protein builds muscle.

> 8 oz. almond milk *or* water
> 8 oz. coconut water
> ½ C organic cherries (frozen)
> 1 orange, peeled
> 2 Tbsp. hemp protein
> 1 Tbsp. green powder
> 3 C mixed greens of choice

Blend and enjoy!

Mrs. Hulk

Thanks for the recipe, NutriMom!

This is a wheatgrass smoothie that is a little different but I love it for variety. I think the ginger and lemon juice is what makes it.

> 1 C cold water
> ½ oz. wheatgrass
> 1 small slice ginger
> juice of ½ lemon
> 1 apple, cored
> 2 peaches *or* 1 mango (can be frozen)
> 1 frozen banana

Blend until smooth.

"Peary" Smooth Smoothie

Thanks for the recipe, Ondyena O.!

> pears
> bananas
> spinach
> water

Blend and enjoy!

Über Berry Green Smoothie

Thanks for the recipe, Pam!

Recently my 16-year-old son was diagnosed with Crohn's disease. When he was in bad flare-up mode, there weren't many things he could eat that didn't bother him. So he made up his own green smoothie recipe.

1 C organic açaí berry juice
2 large kale leaves (no stems)
¼ C coconut milk *or* small container of yogurt
1 scoop vanilla protein powder
½ banana
½ bag frozen mixed berries (strawberries, blueberries, raspberries)

Blend and enjoy! Also good frozen as a popsicle!

Muddy Buddy Smoothie

Thanks for the recipe, Patsy S.!

This is one I drink most often, but it varies a little depending what greens or veggies I use. But the one thing that makes it different is that I use raw chocolate, so it pretty much tastes like a chocolate smoothie.

1 medium kale leaf
1 medium collard green leaf
⅓ avocado
¼ C cashews
1 tsp. flax seeds
2 generous tsp. raw chocolate (very high in antioxidants)
3 tsp. agave (or sweetener of choice)
1 large frozen banana, cut into pieces
water *or* almond milk, to 1" of top of the mixture
optional: 1 small disk fresh ginger, about ⅛" thick x ½" diameter (good for digestion)

Blend well and enjoy

Note: You can use any greens you like. Sometimes I add carrot, celery, romaine, or cucumber. It doesn't matter much what veggies you use. Because of the chocolate, it will taste like a chocolate smoothie. If I have made almond milk, I use some of the pulp in the smoothie.

Adelaide's Blueberry Blast
Thanks for the recipe, Phoebe M.!

I love this smoothie for kids. The color of the blueberries and the sweetness of the bananas make it so my kids have no idea they are consuming so much spinach and kale. My 22-month-old says, "More blueberry to drink please!"

1 C kale
1 C spinach
1 C fresh or frozen blueberries
1-2 frozen bananas
1 C water
2 Tbsp. flaxseed oil

Blend all ingredients. So simple but so yummy!

Everyday Green Smoothie
Thanks for the recipe, Rachel M.!

5 kale leaves
2 C baby spinach
1 banana
½ C blueberries
¼ C strawberries
12 oz. plain, fat-free yogurt
1 Good Belly Juice probiotic
2 Tbsp. flaxseed oil

Blend and enjoy!

Carolyn's Smoothie
Thanks for the recipe, Raechel M.!

parsley
spinach
lettuce
cucumber
carrot
lime
ginger
apple

Blend and enjoy!

Peachy Green Smoothie

Thanks for the recipe, Rebecca H.!

Makes about 2 quarts

spinach (enough to fill blender about half way)
several fresh, ripe peaches
2 fresh carrots, chopped (include green carrot tops if you have them)
1-2 dashes cinnamon
1 small squirt liquid stevia
ice cubes
1 C water

Blend and enjoy!

Berry Green Pomegranate

Thanks for the recipe, Rick M.!

4 oz. pomegranate juice (I use POM brand)
¼ C blueberries
¼ C raspberries
¼ C blackberries
6 strawberries (with tops left on)
1 large kale leaf
1 large red leaf lettuce leaf
1 small handful baby spinach
ice (enough for desired thickness)
optional: 1 tsp. chia seeds
optional: 1 packet stevia (if berries are in season, they will give enough
    sweetness)

Blend and enjoy!

Mega-Marathon Mix

Thanks for the recipe, Robin B.!

The smoothie was the perfect way to start the Seattle Rock-n-Roll Marathon and kept all of us going for hours.

3 bananas
1 C blueberries
1 C strawberries
1 apple
1 peeled orange
½ avocado
1 carrot
several handfuls baby spinach (any greens would do)
1 C plain yogurt
water (to desired consistency)

Blend and enjoy!

Runner's Respite

Thanks for the recipe, Robin B.!

The race went well, and after we splurged on post-race food, we came home and I made the following smoothie.

1 peeled cucumber
2 oranges
1 celery stalk
1-2 C pineapple
several handfuls spinach and chard
1 carrot
water (to make desired consistency)
optional: ice (only if not using frozen fruit)

Blend and enjoy!

Super-Charged Smoothie
Thanks for the recipe, Sandy I.!

I came up with this mixture as a quick and easy breakfast that I can make and clean up in about 5 or 10 minutes from start to finish—then I have a large tumbler of nice, cold nourishment to drink as I drive to work in the morning. I arrive refreshed, energized, and ready for whatever the day has for me.

1 oz. Açaí Blend pure juice
1 kiwi, peeled and quartered
1 small peach, pitted and quartered
1 small Fuji apple, cored and quartered (with peel)
3 large strawberries (with stems)
1 handful fresh spinach
1 Tbsp. wheat germ
½ banana, peeled (good if frozen)
1 C ice cubes or crushed ice

Place items in a BlendTec blender in the order listed.

Tip: If you want the smoothie thinner, you can add a little pomegranate juice.

Cash's Smoothie

Thanks for the recipe, Sarah V.!

> 1 C cold water
> spinach, collard greens, and kale until above the 4-cup mark (with the water)
> 1 banana
> 2 Tbsp. golden flax seeds
> 5 huge frozen strawberries
> ½ - ¾ C frozen blueberries

Blend and enjoy!

Easter Smoothie

Thanks for the recipe, Shauna!

> 3-4 big kale leaves
> 1-2 bananas
> 3 dates
> ½ C strawberries
> ½ - 1 C water *or* ice
> *optional*: 1 handful blueberries

Ok
added 2T cocoa powder
than the berries.

Blend and enjoy!

> *Tip:* I use kale instead of spinach, as I found that the spinach was more acidic and made us feel more bloated. Kale was more alkaline, and the bloating went away! Also, if you have too many greens growing in your garden, cut and wash them, then blend them up with a little water. Pour them into ice cube trays and freeze them, then store them in a plastic bag in the freezer for winter use!

My Favorite Smoothie Combination

Thanks for the recipe, Silvia A.!

8-12 oz. water

½ pineapple, peeled and cut into large chunks (include the core—great enzymes!)

1 medium bunch cilantro, including stems

2-3 C greens (spinach or kale)

1 apple

1 tsp. dulse

optional: agave, to sweeten (but with a sweet pineapple, nothing else is usually needed)

Blend and enjoy!

Tip: Cut other half of pineapple into chunks and freeze for another day

Belly Bliss Green Smoothie

Thanks for the recipe, Stacy K.!

This drink is sweet and refreshing and is literally the creamiest smoothie I've ever had. A beautiful pale green, it's like velvet in a cup! I've been belly-blissing for almost a week and am feeling lighter, cleaner, and more energetic every day.

Makes 2-4 servings (depending on how much you drink at a sitting)

½ ripe avocado, cut into chunks

½ small (or ¼ large) very ripe honeydew melon, cut into chunks

2-3 small "pickling" cucumbers (or 1 small American cucumber), peeled and cut into chunks

1 very large handful green leaf lettuce (about 4 leaves) or any dark leafy greens

approx. ½" piece fresh ginger, squeezed through a garlic press or mashed and finely minced

Blend ingredients together (they're so soft, a hand blender works fine) and serve!

Carroty Fresh

Thanks for the recipe, Sue K.!

> 1½ C water
> ½ C dates
> 1 medium carrot
> 1 large handful fresh spinach
> 1 apple
> 1 banana
> 1 large handful collard greens and Swiss chard
> blueberries or strawberries to fill 1-quart blender

Blend until smooth.

> *Tip:* I add 1 Tbsp. ground flax seeds to 16-oz. glass before drinking.

Newbie Smoothie

Thanks for the recipe, Suzanne!

I always give this one to introduce newbies.

Serves 1 adult

> 1 banana
> 1 cold orange
> approx. 1 C frozen blueberries or strawberries
> approx. 3 C spinach (experiment with different greens such as rainbow chard,
> kale, etc.).

Blend. Add ice cubes if you are using fresh berries.

Energy Boost

Thanks for the recipe, Suzanne S.!

Green smoothies have improved my mood, my skin, and my general nutrition. I still get a lot of rude comments from people around me, but I honestly get an energy boost when I drink one in the morning.

1 C carrot juice
3-4 big kale leaves
3-4 big collard green leaves (or Swiss chard or other greens)
1 C frozen spinach (Trader Joe's has pesticide-free spinach in the frozen foods)
1 frozen banana broken into pieces
1 pinch stevia
1 C frozen mixed berries

Mix first three ingredients on "Smoothie" cycle adding water as necessary to keep blending. Add in spinach, banana, stevia, and more water, and blend on "Smoothie" cycle again. Add mixed berries and blend to consistency desired. I use up to 12 oz. water to keep this a soft-serve consistency. It becomes more liquid through the day.

"Brady" Green Smoothie

Thanks for the recipe, Tammy A.!

2 big handfuls spinach
2 rounded Tbsp. flax seeds
1 banana
1 C strawberries
⅔ C blueberries
2 C water
1 C ice

Blend and enjoy!

Jason's Morning Charge

Thanks for the recipe, Tammy G.!

2 C water
½ fresh pineapple
1 apple
2 kale stalks (take out the stem)
½ - 1 C berries
2 Tbsp. coconut oil
4 Tbsp. hemp hearts
optional: agave nectar

Mix in blender and drink.

Yoda Soda

Thanks for the recipe, Tiffany C.!

This is a real kid-pleaser!

2 collard green leaves
2 C spinach
8 strawberries
1½ bananas
½ C frozen blueberries
1 orange

Blend all ingredients together.

Darth Vader Juice

Thanks for the recipe, Tiffany C.!

> 1 kale leaf
> 1 collard greens leaf
> 1 chard leaf
> 1 C spinach
> 1 C frozen berries
> 1½ frozen bananas
> 1 apple
> 1 orange
> ½ tsp. stevia

Blend and enjoy!

Give Me a Boost

Thanks for the recipe, Tracie H.!

> big bunch kale
> ½ bunch parsley
> 2 oz. frozen açaí juice
> 1 C blueberries
> ½ apple
> 1 C coconut kefir
> 2 Tbsp. hemp seeds
> *optional*: 1 tsp. bee pollen (if it's allergy season)
> *optional*: 1 tsp. maca powder (good for the adrenals)

Blend and enjoy!

Lemon-Lime Coconut Smoothie

Thanks for the recipe, Tracy L.!

> 1 young Thai coconut
>
> ½ - 1 avocado (depending on size), peeled and pitted
>
> ½ - 1 cucumber (depending on size), cut into large chunks (remove peel if desired—we peel just half to keep some of the greens, but not too much)
>
> ⅔ C fresh lemon juice (approx. 3 lemons)
>
> ⅓ C fresh lime juice (approx. 2 limes)
>
> 5-6 pieces ice
>
> stevia (to taste—our favorite is vanilla creme flavor, SweetLeaf brand)
>
> *optional*: 2 C raw spinach (for greens and smoother texture; doesn't affect flavor)

Open the coconut and put its water in a bowl. Scrape out coconut meat and put in the blender. Add avocado, cucumber, ice, lemon and lime juice, and optional spinach. Blend and pulse, then gradually add coconut water and blend to desired consistency. Add stevia to taste (start with about ⅓ of the dropper filled, then add maybe 2-3 drops at a time as it is very strong and much sweeter than sugar).

For a colder, thicker smoothie, freeze 5-6 ice cubes' worth of the coconut water, and then when making the smoothie, use the frozen cubes and replenish for the next smoothie.

We only have a regular blender, but with a BlendTec or other high-powered blender, I'm sure you could skip peeling the cucumber and also use the whole lemons and limes. If you do this, you might want to add a bit more stevia.

> *Tip:* We save time by processing a bunch of the young coconuts at once and freezing them in pint jars, then placing 1 jar in the fridge the night before we'll make the smoothie. This is about the same quantity of coconut milk as 1 coconut.

Piñata Colada Smoothie

Thanks for the recipe, Trisha B.!

> 1 C coconut milk
>
> 2-3 C fresh organic baby spinach
>
> ½ C frozen pineapple
>
> ½ C frozen mango
>
> 1 tsp. vanilla flavoring

Blend all together and pour into smoothie cups, then sprinkle coconut on top and place a pineapple wedge on the rim.

Elise's Juice

Thanks for the recipe, Vicki S.!

I don't really measure anything...so when I say 1 C, that is a guess.

1-2 carrots
2 handfuls spinach (maybe 2 C)
1 C romaine lettuce
1 C yellow squash
¼ C celery
2 C bok choy
1-2 kale leaves
1 C blueberries
1 apple (with most of the core)
1 banana
1 slice avocado
fresh ginger (size of little fingertip)
juice of 1 fresh lemon (I squeeze in the seeds, too)
1 C water
1½ C ice

Blend until smooth.

Elise's Pineapple Delight

Thanks for the recipe, Vicki S.!

approx. ½ fresh pineapple
1 banana (great if frozen)
1 slice fresh ginger (about the size of the tip of your little finger—about ¼" slice)
1 tsp. vanilla
2-4 handfuls fresh spinach (to taste, even more if you want!)
1 C water and ice (add more water if you want it thinner)
optional: Sometimes I also add carrot and squash (about ½ C each), kiwi, apple, and fresh mint

Throw it all in your BlendTec and push the "Whole Fruit" button. Yummy!

Can't Live without It
Thanks for the recipe, Vicky!

1 handful parsley
1 handful spinach
1 celery stalk
ginger root, to taste
½ lemon
water, to desired consistency

Blend and enjoy!

Mango Peach Supreme
Thanks for the recipe, Wendy P.!

1¾ C water
blender-and-a-half of spinach
1 mango
2 frozen bananas
1 large handful frozen peaches
½ C frozen raspberries

Blend spinach about 60 seconds, then add water and fruit and blend about 90 seconds.

Spring Green Smoothie
Thanks for the recipe, Wendy S.!

1 C water
2 bananas
1 orange
¾ - 1 whole Meyer lemon (peel, seeds, and all)
1 celery stalk
2-second pour of flaxseed oil
10 chunks (approx.) pineapple
2 large kale leaves
2-3 huge handfuls spinach
1 sprinkle of stevia *or* ½ Bosc pear *or* about ¼ C pineapple juice

Blend and enjoy!

Green Smoothie 3

Thanks for the recipe, Willy!

This is the smoothie I've been drinking for a very long time and I never tire of it. This is soooo filling, and I have tons of energy after drinking this!

½ C oats (wheatberries or any other sprouted grain works too)

¼ C any nuts or seeds

1 Tbsp. flaxseed oil *or* 2 Tbsp. flax meal

1 C kefir

½ C unsweetened almond milk *or* coconut milk *or* coconut water

1 banana

1 C frozen blueberries

1 handful spinach and/or kale

1 scoop super green food

½" piece fresh ginger (powder works too)

1 dash cinnamon, nutmeg, and/or vanilla

optional: 1 packet stevia *or* 1 Tbsp. local raw honey

Blend & enjoy!

Tropical Delight

Thanks for the recipe, Yvonne F.!

½ pineapple

1 mango

1 large banana

2 huge handfuls spinach

1 young Thai coconut (meat and liquid)

water (if coconut does not provide enough liquid to blend to desired consistency)

Blend and enjoy!

The Kissed Toad

Thanks for the recipe, Zoe!

My BEST green smoothie is very delicious! I am diabetic, so have to watch sugar.

¼ - ½ C apple
½ C berries
1-2 C any nut or seed milk
1 Tbsp. ground sesame seeds
1 Tbsp. ground flax seeds
2 scoops protein powder
1 tsp. Spirulina
optional: 1 handful kale
optional: 1 handful walnuts
optional: local honey *or* stevia

Blend both flax seeds and sesame seeds together for 2-3 min. Toss in the rest of the ingredients and blend.

Adrienne (UT)

Aengus (PA)

Audrey (NC)

Lily, Asher (TX)

Bunnies LOVE Green Smoothies!

Blaise (UT)

Briella (UT)

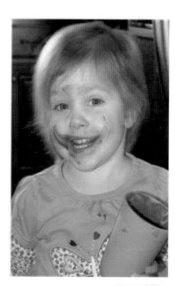
Bailey (ID)

Charles (Australia)

Camerion, Isaac, Macey (WA)

Charlie (NC)

Clover (ID)

Elena (UT)

Ella (VA)

Evangeline (WA)

Elijah, Emily (CA)

Heath (TN)

Holly (NM)

Isaiah and Mom (UT)

Ian (IN)

Jaxon, Ashton (UT)

Jake (OR)

Jakob, Gracy, Lexy, Ethynn (NV)

Jack (CA)

Justin (Canada)

Jessica (UT)

Jillian (UT)

Justin (GA)

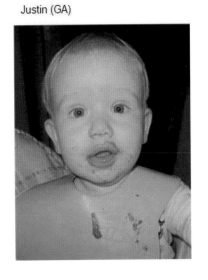

Kevin (UT)

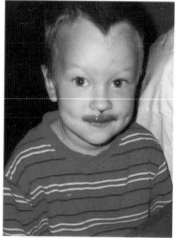

Kiya (MI)

Konner and Mom (United Kingdom)

Karys (Canada)

Madison (UT)

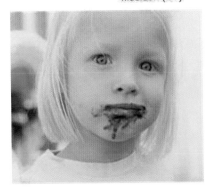

Madison, Heath (NE)

Luz (UT)

Madelyn (UT)

Manny (UT)

Mia, Lexi (Switzerland)

Mason (UT)

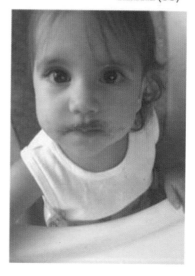

Marcella (SC)

Sarah, Jessica (UT)

Peyton, Avery (FL)

Ruby (MO)

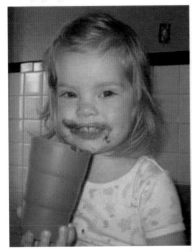

Savannah, Jake, Zach (UT)

Syrus the Dog

Shannon (CA)

Teja (UT)

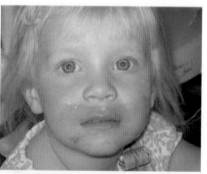

Tessa (CA)

Shoshanna, Josiah (NH)

Robyn's youngest, Tennyson, and one of his favorite green smoothies.

Robyn enjoying a green smoothie on her front porch.

Robyn's Smoothies

Any Season

Super Simple Starter Smoothie

3 C water/ice
½ tsp. stevia
spinach, added until blended mixture reaches 6-cup line
2 oranges
2 bananas, frozen in chunks
1 apple or pear
frozen mixed berries added to 9-cup line

Blend first three ingredients until smooth. Add remaining ingredients and blend until smooth. Serve immediately or refrigerate for up to 24 hours and shake well before serving.

Sweet Veggielicious

3 C water/ice
1 large English cucumber
1 large carrot
1 celery stalk
beet greens, added until blended mixture reaches 6-cup line
½ tsp. nutmeg
2 Tbsp. raw honey (local, if possible)
2 large, ripe pears
3 C frozen mixed berries
1 banana, frozen in chunks

Blend first four ingredients until smooth. Add remaining ingredients and blend until smooth. Serve immediately or refrigerate for up to 24 hours and shake well before serving.

Salad Smoothie

2 C water/ice
1 cucumber, washed and peeled
1 celery stalk, quartered
1 large carrot, quartered
1 red, orange, or yellow bell pepper
3 large, ripe tomatoes
1 large handful romaine, green leaf, or red leaf lettuce
⅛ yellow onion
1 pinch sea salt
freshly ground pepper to taste
tabasco or hot sauce to taste

Blend all ingredients until very smooth. Serve immediately.

Chocoholics' Choice

My kids love this one!

3 C water/ice
½ vanilla bean
2 large chard or collard leaves
red leaf lettuce, added until blended mixture reaches 6-cup line
¼ C cacao nibs or powdered chocolate
2 Granny Smith apples
2 mangos, peeled and pits removed
2 bananas, frozen in chunks
½ C almond butter *or* ⅔ C raw almonds (puréed with water as a first step)
8 pitted dates

Blend first four ingredients until smooth. Add remaining ingredients and blend until smooth. Serve immediately or refrigerate for up to 24 hours and shake well before serving.

Winter

Holiday Green Smoothie

Forget the power struggle over getting your kids to eat their greens. Give them this smoothie and they will be begging for more! High in vitamin C, this smoothie will help you fight off winter colds.

> 4 persimmons
> 1-2 frozen bananas
> 2 C almond milk
> ½ C plain kefir
> ½ avocado
> 2 C spinach
> 2 C kale
> 1 Tbsp. chia seeds
> *optional*: 1-3 tsp. agave (raw, organic)

Blend all ingredients in a high-powered blender for about 1-2 min.

Black Chia-licious

> 3¼ C water/ice
> 1 Tbsp. chia seeds
> spinach, added until blended mixture reaches 6-cup line
> 2 Tbsp. raw honey (local, if possible)
> 4 black plums, pits removed
> 2 bananas, frozen in chunks
> 3 C frozen mixed berries
> *optional*: a few dashes of hot sauce, cayenne, or cinnamon

Blend first three ingredients until smooth. Add all other ingredients and blend well. Serve immediately or refrigerate for up to 24 hours and shake well before serving.

Pooh's Pollen Potion

Bee pollen is famous for its aphrodisiac qualities as well as its ability to enhance your energy and many other health benefits. Raw local honey may help eliminate or reduce seasonal allergies.

2¾ C water/ice

2 Tbsp. bee pollen

2 Tbsp. raw honey (local, if possible)

1 tsp. pumpkin pie spice

spinach, added until blended mixture reaches 6-cup line

2 C persimmons, chopped

1 banana, frozen in chunks

2 Gala or Jonagold apples

2 C frozen marionberries

Blend first five ingredients until smooth. Add remaining ingredients and blend until smooth. Serve immediately or refrigerate for up to 24 hours and shake well before serving.

Dandelion Doodleberry Juice

2¾ C water

2 large stalks celery

¼ whole lemon (including peel)

2" fresh ginger, peeled

4 C dandelion greens

spinach, added until blended mixture reaches 6-cup line

2 apples

1 pear

1 banana, frozen in chunks

frozen berries added and blended until container is very full

Blend first six ingredients until smooth. Add fruit and blend until smooth. Serve immediately or refrigerate for up to 24 hours and shake well before serving.

Ginger Celery Thirstee

2¾ C water/ice
1-2" fresh ginger, peeled
¼ C agave (raw, organic)
2 large handfuls arugula
2 celery stalks
1 ripe avocado
spinach, added until mixture reaches 6-cup line
2 apples
2 bananas, frozen in chunks
frozen mixed berries, added until container is very full

Blend first seven ingredients in the order listed. Then add the fruit and blend until very smooth. Serve immediately or refrigerate for up to 24 hours and shake well before serving.

You Can't Tell There's Brussels Sprouts in Here!

3 C water/ice
10 large Brussels sprouts
spinach, added until blended mixture reaches 6-cup line
2 oranges, peeled
3 C frozen mixed berries
2 bananas, frozen in chunks
½ tsp. stevia

Blend first three ingredients until smooth. Add remaining ingredients and blend until smooth. Serve immediately or refrigerate for up to 24 hours and shake well before serving.

Green Asia

This recipe has you going to your local Asian market for an inexpensive variety of new greens that you may have never used before.

> 2¼ C water/ice
> 8 C loose bok choy and yu choy (coarsely chopped)
> 1 C Chinese celery
> 1-2 C bean sprouts
> ¼ C agave (raw, organic)
> 4 tangelos
> 1 large plantain
> 2 apples (any kind)
> 3 C frozen mixed berries

Blend first three ingredients until smooth. Add remaining ingredients and purée until smooth. Best if served immediately (sprouts oxidize and lose nutrition quickly when blended)—or pour in glass jars and refrigerate for up to 24 hours and shake well before serving.

Sunflower Shower

> 2¾ C water/ice
> 2 oz. sunflower greens (sprouts)
> romaine or Bibb lettuce, added until blended mixture reaches 6-cup line
> ¼ whole lime (including peel)
> 3 plums, pits removed
> 2 bananas, frozen in chunks
> 2 apples
> frozen berries added until container is very full

Blend first three ingredients until smooth. Add remaining ingredients and blend until smooth. Serve immediately or refrigerate for up to 24 hours and shake well before serving.

Kumquat Slush

2¾ C water/ice

1 C broccoli sprouts

spinach, added until blended mixture reaches 6-cup line

1 C kumquats (including skin)

3 bananas, frozen in chunks

3 C frozen mixed berries

⅓ C agave (raw, organic)

Blend first three ingredients until smooth, then add remaining ingredients and blend again until smooth. Serve immediately or refrigerate for up to 24 hours and shake well before serving.

Collard Cooler

2½ C water/ice

4 collard green leaves

1 (10-oz.) bag baby spinach

5 oranges or tangerines

1 banana, frozen in chunks

3 C frozen mixed berries

¼ whole lemon (including peel)

¼ C agave (raw, organic)

Blend first three ingredients well. Add remaining ingredients and purée until smooth. Serve immediately or refrigerate for up to 24 hours and shake well before serving.

Orange Oobleck

4 C beet greens, coarsely chopped (wild/unsprayed or found in health food store)

½ tsp. stevia

¼ C frozen orange juice (freshly squeezed and frozen in ice cube trays—2 large ice cubes is ¼ C)

watercress, added until blended mixture reaches 6-cup line

2 oranges

2 bananas, frozen in chunks

frozen berries added until container is very full

Blend first four ingredients until smooth. Add fruit and blend until smooth. Serve immediately or refrigerate for up to 24 hours and shake well before serving.

Parsley Perfection

2¾ C water/ice
2 C parsley
spinach, added until blended mixture reaches 6-cup line
¼ C raw honey (local, if possible)
½ tsp. ground cinnamon
1 large pink grapefruit, peeled
2 pears
2 bananas, frozen in chunks
¼ whole lemon (including peel)
2 C frozen mixed berries

Blend first four ingredients until smooth. Add remaining ingredients and blend until smooth. Serve immediately or refrigerate for up to 24 hours and shake well before serving.

Note: This recipe becomes stronger tasting if not consumed immediately.

Black Brew

2¾ C water/ice
2 celery stalks
5 large leaves black (Lacinato) kale
2 Tbsp. agave (raw, organic)
spinach, added until blended mixture reaches 6-cup line
2 Tbsp. flaxseed oil
2 C chopped fresh pineapple (optionally frozen)
1 orange
2 C blackberries
2 bananas, frozen in chunks

Blend first six ingredients until smooth. Add fruit and blend until smooth. Serve immediately or refrigerate for up to 24 hours and shake well before serving.

Pom-Poms Please

2¾ C water/ice
5 large curly kale leaves
spinach, added until blended mixture reaches 6-cup line
¼ C agave (raw, organic)
4 tangerines *or* 2 oranges
1 banana, frozen in chunks
seeds of 1 large pomegranate (1 C or more)
2 Granny Smith apples
2 C mixed frozen berries

Blend first three ingredients until smooth, then add remaining ingredients and blend again until smooth. Serve immediately or refrigerate for up to 24 hours and shake well before serving.

Fennel Free-for-All

2¾ C water/ice
4 whole key limes (including peel)
2 C anise (fennel) greens
spinach, added until blended mixture reaches 6-cup line
3 d'Anjou pears
2 bananas, frozen in chunks
2 C frozen berries (any kind)
1 tsp. stevia

Blend first four ingredients until smooth. Add remaining ingredients and blend until smooth. Serve immediately or refrigerate for up to 24 hours and shake well before serving.

Lettuce Be Green

1 C water/ice
1¾ C water
1 head red leaf lettuce, washed
kale, added until blended mixture reaches 6-cup line
2 whole key limes (including peel)
1 avocado, peeled and pit removed
2 Granny Smith apples
1 banana, frozen in chunks
4 C frozen mixed berries
¼ C raw honey (local, if possible)

Blend first four ingredients until smooth. Add fruit and honey and blend until smooth. Serve immediately for best results or refrigerate up to 24 hours and shake well before serving.

Blast of Broccoli

2¾ C water/ice
⅔ tsp. stevia
2 C broccoli (florets and/or stems) or broccoli rabe (found in Italian or Asian markets)
spinach, added until blended mixture reaches 5-cup line
1 orange, peeled and quartered
2 C pineapple, chopped
2 bananas, frozen in chunks
2 C frozen mixed berries

Blend first four ingredients until smooth. Add fruit and blend again until smooth. Serve immediately or refrigerate for up to 24 hours and shake well before serving.

Green and Purple

2¾ C water/ice

1–2 heads green leaf lettuce (or enough added until blended mixture reaches 6-cup line)

⅛ - ¼ whole lemon (including peel)

½ tsp. stevia

2 C pineapple, frozen in chunks

2 apples

2 bananas, frozen in chunks

2 C frozen mixed berries

Blend first three ingredients until smooth. Add stevia and fruit and blend until smooth. Serve immediately for best results or refrigerate up to 24 hours and shake well before serving.

Lemon Ginger Splash

2¾ C water/ice

4 C cabbage (any type)

spinach, added until blended mixture reaches 6-cup line

¼ whole lemon (including peel)

1" fresh ginger, peeled

6 large dates *or* ⅓ C chopped dates (rinsed)

3 large d'Anjou pears

3 C frozen mixed berries

If possible, soak dates in water for 30 minutes. Blend first six ingredients until smooth. Add pears and berries and blend again until smooth. Serve immediately for best results or refrigerate up to 24 hours and shake well before serving.

Carrot Top

 2¾ C water/ice
 greens from 6 carrots
 spinach, added until blended mixture reaches 6-cup line
 ¼ C agave (raw, organic)
 2 pears
 2 oranges
 1 banana
 1 C frozen strawberries

Blend first three ingredients for 1 min., then add remaining ingredients and blend until smooth. Serve immediately or refrigerate for up to 24 hours and shake well before serving.

Spring

Glorious Goji

    3½ C water/ice
    1 C dried (or fresh) goji berries (if fresh, decrease water by ½ C)
    3 large handfuls spring greens
    2 handfuls arugula
    spinach, added until blended mixture reaches 6-cup line
    ⅓ C agave (raw, organic)
    2 bananas, frozen in chunks
    1 C frozen blackberries
    12 large frozen strawberries
    3 oranges

Soak goji berries in the water for the smoothie 30-60 min. in advance. Then add all greens and blend until smooth. Add agave and fruit and blend again until smooth. Serve immediately or refrigerate for up to 24 hours and shake well before serving.

Sexy Springtime Surprise

Maca is a energy-boosting power food from a root vegetable prized by ancient Incans for improving sexual desire and performance.

    3 C water/ice
    mixed spring greens, added until blended mixture reaches 4-cup line
    chard, added until blended mixture reaches 6-cup line
    ¼ C maca root powder
    ½ tsp. lemon-flavored liquid stevia
    ¼ whole lemon (including peel)
    2 C pineapple
    2 bananas, frozen in chunks
    4 C frozen berries

Blend first two ingredients until smooth, then add chard, blending until smooth. Add remaining ingredients and blend until smooth. Serve immediately for best results or refrigerate up to 24 hours and shake well before serving.

Summer

Kool Kale

2¾ C water/ice
spinach, added until blended mixture reaches 4-cup line
curly kale, added until blended mixture reaches 6-cup line
¼ C agave (raw, organic)
3 C frozen mixed berries
4 nectarines or peaches
2 bananas, frozen in chunks

Blend first two ingredients well, then add kale, blending well. Add agave and fruit and blend until smooth. Serve immediately or refrigerate for up to 24 hours and shake well before serving.

Charnana Cantalapple

This is good any season, but is best in late summer.

2¾ C water/ice
4 large handfuls spinach
rainbow swiss chard leaves and stems, added until blended mixture reaches 6-cup line
2 bananas, frozen in chunks
3 C frozen mixed berries
½ cantaloupe, including seeds
2 Gala or Braeburn apples (or enough to make blender container very full)
¼ C agave (raw, organic)

Blend first three ingredients until smooth. Add fruit and agave and blend until smooth. Serve immediately or refrigerate for up to 24 hours and shake well before serving.

Cress Crush

2¾ C water/ice

1 bunch watercress

3 kale leaves (any kind)

spring greens, added until blended mixture reaches 6-cup line

¼ whole lemon (including peel)

5 ripe apricots (optionally frozen in chunks)

2 ripe peaches (optionally frozen in chunks)

1 banana, frozen in chunks

1 C blueberries

Blend first four ingredients until smooth, then add fruit and blend again until smooth. Serve immediately or refrigerate for up to 24 hours and shake well before serving.

MmmmmmmMustard!

2¾ C water/ice

2 large mustard greens leaves (and stems), coarsely chopped

4 C romaine, coarsely chopped

spinach, added until blended mixture reaches 6-cup line

⅔ tsp. powdered stevia

2 bananas, frozen in chunks

16 oz. frozen blackberries

1 small papaya (including seeds, peel removed)

3 C melon (any kind), preferably frozen in chunks

Blend first four ingredients until smooth, then add remaining ingredients and blend again until smooth. Serve immediately or refrigerate for up to 24 hours and shake well before serving.

Summertime Picnic Punch

    1 C water
    4 C watermelon chunks
    4 turnip green leaves (and stems), coarsely chopped
    spring greens *or* green leaf lettuce, added until blended mixture reaches 6-cup
        line
    ¼ C agave (raw, organic)
    2 peaches
    1½ C fresh (or 2 C frozen) raspberries
    2 bananas, frozen in chunks

Blend first four ingredients until smooth. Add the other ingredients and blend again until very smooth. Serve immediately or refrigerate for up to 24 hours and shake well before serving.

Weedy Whatnot

    2¾ C water/ice
    4 C radish, carrot, strawberry, and/or beet tops, washed very well
    1 C wild greens (like purslane, milkweed, morning glory, or thistle)
    spinach, added until blended mixture reaches 6-cup line
    ½ tsp stevia
    3 C cantaloupe *or* honeydew melon (including seeds, rind removed)
    2 bananas, frozen in chunks
    2 C frozen mixed berries

Blend first four ingredients until very smooth. Add stevia and fruit and blend until smooth. Serve immediately or refrigerate for up to 24 hours and shake well before serving.

Ironman Smoothie

2¾ C water/ice

4 C kale *or* collard greens, coarsely chopped

spinach, added until blended mixture reaches 6-cup line

¼ C unsulfured molasses

1 (12-oz.) bag frozen (or 3 C fresh) pitted cherries

2 bananas, frozen in chunks

12 apricots, pitted

Blend first three ingredients until smooth. Add remaining ingredients and blend again until smooth. Serve immediately or refrigerate for up to 24 hours and shake well before serving.

Melon-Seed Melange

It looks very green, but it's tasty! These ingredients are best when they're available in the very late summer or early fall.

¼ C raw, organic agave

2 C water

2-3 C kale (any kind)

1 C chopped parsley

spinach, added until blended mixture reaches 6-cup line

4 C cantaloupe, including all the seeds, etc., in the center (rind removed)

2 bananas, frozen in chunks

12 medium-to-large frozen strawberries

Blend first five ingredients until very smooth. Add remaining ingredients and blend again until smooth. Serve immediately or refrigerate for up to 24 hours and shake well before serving.

Green Yogurt

2½ C water/ice

1 C yogurt *or* kefir (plain, unflavored)

2 chard leaves, including stems

2 collard green leaves, including stems

spinach, added until blended mixture reaches 6½-cup line

⅓ C agave (raw, organic)

2 C peaches

2 C blueberries

2 bananas, frozen in chunks

2 C melon (any kind)

Blend first six ingredients until smooth. Add remaining ingredients and blend again until smooth. Serve immediately or refrigerate for up to 24 hours and shake well before serving.

Thunder Down Under

3 C water/ice

6 medium chard *or* collard green leaves (and stems)

spinach, added until blended mixture reaches 6-cup line

6 kiwis, peeled

1 banana, frozen in chunks

2 pears

3 C frozen berries (or enough to make blender container very full)

2 Tbsp. unsulfured molasses

Blend first three ingredients until smooth. Add fruit and molasses and blend again until smooth. Serve immediately for best results or refrigerate up to 24 hours and shake well before serving.

Ginger and Mary Ann

2¾ C water/ice
2 large spears fresh aloe vera, cut from the plant (or ¼ C bottled)
4 large turnip green leaves
spinach, added until blended mixture reaches 6-cup line
1–2" fresh ginger, peeled
2 large tart green apples
2 bananas, frozen in chunks
3 C frozen blueberries
¼ C agave (raw, organic)

Blend first five ingredients until smooth. Add fruit and agave and blend again until smooth. Serve immediately for best results or refrigerate up to 24 hours and shake well before serving.

Seaworthy Smoothie

3+ C water/ice
2 large handfuls arugula
¼ C arame *or* 1 raw nori sheet (iodine-rich sea vegetables)
spinach, added until blended mixture reaches 6-cup line
2 C pineapple, preferably frozen in chunks
2 bananas, frozen in chunks
2 C frozen blueberries, blackberries, or mixed berries
1 apple or pear
½ tsp. stevia

Blend first four ingredients until smooth. Add fruit and stevia and blend again until smooth. Serve immediately for best results or refrigerate up to 24 hours and shake well before serving.

Carroty Concoction

2¾ C water/ice
2 stalks celery
2 carrots
romaine lettuce, added until blended mixture reaches 6-cup line
½ tsp. stevia
1 C melon (any kind)
8 apricots (preferably halved and frozen) *or* 4 peaches
2 bananas, frozen in chunks
2 C frozen mixed berries

Blend first four ingredients until smooth. Add stevia and fruit and blend again until smooth. Serve immediately for best results or refrigerate up to 24 hours and shake well before serving.

Buttery Brew

2¾ C water/ice
1 head butter lettuce
½ C broccoli *or* alfalfa sprouts
spinach, added until blended mixture reaches 6-cup line
½ tsp. stevia
2 bananas, frozen in chunks
2 C papaya (including seeds)
2 C frozen blueberries
2 C frozen fruit medley or other fruit (or enough to make blender very full)

Blend the first four ingredients well. Add stevia and fruit and blend again until smooth. Serve immediately for best nutrition (sprouts oxidize quickly) or refrigerate up to 24 hours and shake well before serving.

Spicy Summer

2¾ C water/ice

4 radishes (including green tops), washed well

3 oz. sunflower greens (sprouts)

spinach, added until blended mixture reaches 6-cup line

¼ C chopped dates

½ tsp. cayenne pepper

2 C pineapple, preferably frozen in chunks

3 C strawberries (including green tops)

3 bananas, frozen in chunks

Blend first four ingredients until smooth. Add remaining ingredients and blend again until smooth. Serve immediately for best nutrition (sprouts oxidize quickly) or refrigerate up to 24 hours and shake well before serving.

Pepper-Mint Pollen Potion

2¾ C water/ice

1 orange or yellow bell pepper

1 large celery stalk

¼ whole lemon (including peel)

1 handful fresh mint leaves

spinach, added until blended mixture reaches 6-cup line

¼ C agave (raw, organic)

1 Tbsp. bee pollen

3 peaches

2 C frozen mixed berries

2 C melon (any kind)

1 banana, frozen in chunks

Blend first six ingredients until smooth. Add remaining ingredients and blend again until smooth. Serve immediately or refrigerate for up to 24 hours and shake well before serving.

Razzy Radicchio

> 3 C water/ice
> 2 large handfuls radicchio or red/purple cabbage
> 4 radishes (including green tops), washed well
> spinach, added until blended mixture reaches 6-cup line
> ¼ C raw honey (local, if possible)
> 2 C raspberries
> 3 C strawberries
> 2 bananas, frozen in chunks

Blend first four ingredients until smooth. Add honey and fruit and blend again until smooth. Serve immediately for best results or refrigerate up to 24 hours and shake well before serving.

Cabbage Cocktail

> 3 C water/ice
> 4 C black cabbage
> spinach, added until blended mixture reaches 6-cup line
> ½ tsp. stevia powder
> 2 peaches
> 2 bananas, frozen in chunks
> 8 apricots, pits removed (or equivalent amount of frozen mixed fruit)

Blend first three ingredients until smooth. Add remaining ingredients and blend again until smooth. Serve immediately or refrigerate for up to 24 hours and shake well before serving.

Delicious Dill

2¾ C water/ice
⅓ C fresh dill weed
4 C spring greens
spinach, added until blended mixture reaches 6-cup line
2 Tbsp. raw honey (local, if possible)
⅛ whole lime (including peel)
4 C pitted cherries
2 bananas
2 C frozen mixed berries

Blend first four ingredients until smooth. Add remaining ingredients and blend again until smooth. Serve immediately or refrigerate for up to 24 hours and shake well before serving.

Mondo Mango

2¾ C water/ice
2 stalks chard (any kind), chopped into fourths
spinach, added until blended mixture reaches 6-cup line
2" piece vanilla bean
¼ C agave (raw, organic)
2 large mangos, peeled and cut away from the pit
2 bananas, frozen in chunks
2 C frozen blueberries
½ C yogurt or kefir (plain, nonfat)

Blend first three ingredients until smooth, then add remaining ingredients and blend again until very smooth. Serve immediately for best results or refrigerate up to 24 hours and shake well before serving.

Islander Icee

2¾ C young Thai coconut liquid (and ice)

¼ C agave (raw, organic)

spinach or chard (any kind), added until blended mixture reaches 6-cup line

3 C chopped fresh pineapple, frozen in chunks

1 C young Thai coconut flesh

2 C guanabana fruit or pulp (if you can find it, imported—if not, use any other fruit)

3 bananas, frozen in chunks

Blend first three ingredients until smooth. Add remaining ingredients and blend again until smooth. Serve immediately for best nutrition or refrigerate for up to 24 hours and shake well before serving

Fall

Deep Purple

3¼ C water/ice

1 medium beet, washed well and quartered

¼ medium purple cabbage, cut into chunks

spinach, added until blended mixture reaches 6-cup line

2 Tbsp. raw honey (local, if possible)

2 tart-sweet apples

2 bananas, frozen in chunks

2 C pineapple, frozen in chunks

½ tsp. pumpkin pie spice

Blend first four ingredients for 1 min., then add remaining ingredients and blend until very smooth. Serve immediately or refrigerate up to 24 hours and shake well before serving.

Berry Good

3 C water/ice

green cabbage (or any Asian cabbage), added until blended mixture reaches 6-cup line

4 C frozen mixed berries

2 bananas, frozen in chunks

2 large Bosc pears

¼ C raw agave

Blend first two ingredients until smooth. Add fruit and agave and blend until smooth. Serve immediately or refrigerate up to 24 hours and shake well before serving.